D1302811

Caroline S.
Fairless

Foreword by
Louis Weil

Children at
Worship

Congregations
In Bloom

 CHURCH

Church Publishing
New York

Copyright © 2000, Caroline Fairless
All rights reserved

Library of Congress Cataloging-in-Publication Data

Fairless, Caroline, 1947
        Children at worship:congregations in bloom / Caroline S. Fairless
        p. cm.
        Includes bibliographical references
        ISBN 0898693268 (pbk.)
        Children in public worship—Episcopal Church.
        Worship (Religious education)
BV26.2F35   2000   00-34613
264'.03—dc21   CIP

Church Publishing Incorporated
445 Fifth Avenue
New York, NY 10017

Http://www.churchpublishing.org

5 4 3 2 1

Dedicated
to
Maria Gouyd and the children of Holy Family Church
without whom there would be no
Children at Worship: Congregations in Bloom

Table of Contents

Arrangement:

- This book is arranged in a liturgical order. Think of it as a teaching text for designers of worship, working from the traditional shape of the liturgy.
- Under each chapter heading is a brief synopsis of the chapter's content.

Foreword

Children and the Liturgy: A Perspective

The incorporation of children as members of the worshiping community has been a matter of primary pastoral importance in recent years. It is one dimension of the recovery of the continuing role which Baptism plays in the lives of Christians. In this larger context, there has emerged awareness that the practice of the Baptism of infants is an anomaly if it does not bear fruit in the children's participation in the liturgical life of their parish church. We are reclaiming the insight of the early church that Baptism is not a matter of individual salvation so much as the sign of a person's incorporation into the community whose life is grounded in God's saving action in Jesus Christ. Since the weekly Sunday assembly is normatively the occasion of the celebration of the Holy Eucharist as "the principal act of Christian worship on the Lord's Day" (Book of Common Prayer, 13), it follows that our incorporation through Baptism into the community which celebrates the Eucharist implies that all the baptized members of the parish have a place in that weekly assembly as full participants.

I am emphasizing this fundamental insight because problems have arisen in many parishes as they have attempted to find appropriate ways for the children of the community to participate in a liturgy which has, for centuries, been shaped in accordance with the expectations of an essentially adult gathering of people. In my own observation, the problems which have arisen occur because practical issues have been given first consideration as members try to find ways to incorporate the children. Yet often, with the best of intentions, the parish continues to function with a model of the liturgy in which children have never been present. In other words, the integration of children often runs aground because the often unconscious goal is to maintain the adult model as much as possible. This approach means that the goal is based upon a very limited perspective as to possible solutions other than a modest adaptation of the adult model. In this approach, practical considerations create difficult hurdles, and much attention is given to discussing whether the children should be there for the entire liturgy. If not, then for what part of the liturgy? If they are present for the Liturgy of the Word, then should a brief sermon for children be inserted in addition to the adult sermon? Or should the children be brought in at the Preparation of the Gifts so that they may be present for the Communion rite and receive the eucharistic gifts? Ultimately, of course, all of these questions must be faced, and it is likely that different responses may be developed in different pastoral contexts.

Yet the issue of the integration of children as members of the full worshiping community is an imperative which merits more attention to the grounding in the theology upon which the sacramental actions of Christians are based. For an adequate discernment of this imperative, both the theology and history of the liturgical life of the church work together to suggest that what is needed today is not some minor adaptations of the adult model. In places where children are baptized members of our congregations, as is certainly the case for an overwhelming majority, the appropriate incorporation of children often requires a radical revisioning of the liturgical model itself.

Many of us know from experience that if practical solutions are not grounded in the larger foundation of theology, history, and the pastoral tradition of the church, discussion is often reduced to confrontation. It is quite understandable that, for adults accustomed to liturgies characterized by peace and quiet, a kind of refuge from the stress of daily life, the introduction of children into the assembly, with their active bodies and spontaneous voices, requires a very difficult adjustment. For some people it is an adjustment which they are not prepared to make. And so we make minor adjustments, resulting in the creation of a liturgical model which is not really appropriate to either children or adults. The patch tears the garment. When such a situation exists, experience has shown that often it is pastorally more appropriate to keep the traditional model intact, and to develop a new model at another time on Sunday, a model which emerges from the kind of revisioning which the incorporation of children requires.

Caroline Fairless has enormous experience of such a revisioning of the liturgy from her years of experience as a parish priest in a community where children were highly valued not only for themselves, but for the spirit and gifts which they brought into the liturgical assembly. In *Children at Worship: Congregations in Bloom*, Caroline Fairless shares the insights she has acquired through this experience. My goal in this foreword is to summarize the theological imperatives implicit in her work, to offer a perspective from history of the gradual alienation of children from the liturgical assembly, and to suggest that the victims of that development were not only the children but also the adult community.

The practice of the Baptism of infants, a practice that is normative in the Anglican tradition, raises a number of theological issues. I am not suggesting here that the practice of infant Baptism should be abandoned by the Anglican Communion, but rather that we have not dealt adequately with the effects of the shift in the practice of the church in the fifth century. At that time the emergence of Christendom meant that infants and children were no longer baptized with their parents because their parents themselves had already been baptized as infants. Yet from a theological perspective, the Baptism of infants rests upon the presumed existence of a committed adult community. The children are baptized into the community of adults who profess the Christian faith and who will see that they are nurtured in a context in which they will grow to maturity and, at an appropriate time, profess the faith on their own.

The problem with this is that two very important aspects of the baptismal process, as it was understood in the early church, were the unnecessary victims of the shift to the Baptism of predominantly infant candidates. First there was the loss of the catechumenate, an intense period of preparation and formation. Although models for the catechumenate varied somewhat during the early centuries, its purpose was clear: to confront a person with the consequences in their daily lives of their decision to profess faith in Christ. The catechumenate collapsed under the impact of the shift to infant Baptism and the presumption, perhaps unconscious, that in the context of a Christianized society the goal of the catechumenate would be achieved by a kind of osmosis as one was raised in a Christian family. If that happened at first, it certainly ended with the expansion of the church into northern Europe, into mostly non-urban regions, where the people submitted to Baptism on the basis of the faith-allegiance of the monarch. In this context, in a social situation in which standards of education of any kind, not to mention catechetical formation, were abysmally low, parents could not fulfill such an expectation. They themselves were often little removed from the superstitions of the earlier religious beliefs of their local society. Baptism came to be performed as quickly as possible after birth, and formation for the life of mature faith virtually disappeared.

The second aspect of the baptismal process which fell victim in this new context was the integration of the child—after Baptism—into the sacramental life of the church. In the later medieval period, the lack of Christian formation in the adult society resulted in an alienation of the laity from participation in the Sunday Eucharist. As the priest became increasingly isolated within a clericalized model of presiding, the laity were left with only a passive role at the liturgy. As bishops and other teachers became concerned about this situation, a whole school of allegorical interpretations of the liturgy was developed in order to give the laity some contact with the meaning of the rites through a visual mode in which diverse meanings were applied to each moment of the Mass ritual. This visual mode of participation came to its climax with the introduction of the liturgical custom of the priest elevating the Host at the time of the recitation of the Words of Institution. Eventually this elevation accompanied the Words over the chalice as well, and so emerged as the primary way in which the laity engaged the Eucharist, a devotional practice that completely obscured the meal aspect of the ritual. Perhaps inevitably, the Communion of the laity came to be seen as a non-essential element of the celebration.

It is important for us to take note of this development because in the wake of the marginalization of the Communion of adult laity, and the emergence of the practice of only an annual Communion, the reception of the Eucharistic gifts by children was lost as well. As late as the twelfth century there is evidence that infants continued to receive the sacrament at the time of their Baptism. As an increasingly scrupulous attitude developed with regard to the sacred species, and since infants were often not yet able to eat bread, their baptismal Communion was generally given only in the species of the consecrated wine, with a small amount placed on the lips of the baby from the finger of the deacon. With the general loss of Communion from the chalice by the adult laity, the question arose as to whether it was even appropriate for infants and children to receive the sacrament, and so, in pastoral practice, the giving of Communion to a child for the first time was delayed until they reached what was called "the age of reason."*

In this confluence of theology and history we see, at the very least, that the reduced role of children within the liturgical assembly cannot be seen as "normative" either in the perspective of the church's theology of initiation or of the historical factors which led to the removal of children from the assembly as full communicants by virtue of their Baptism. The issue, of course, is neither merely the presence of children at the Sunday liturgy, nor merely that they should receive Communion. The larger issue is the full integration of children into the worshiping assembly, and the impact of that integration upon the norms of our models of liturgical prayer in our congregations. The fact that the 1979 American Book of Common Prayer authorizes that Holy Baptism "is appropriately administered within the Eucharist as the chief service on a Sunday or other feast" (Book of Common Prayer, 298), strongly suggests not only that we are attempting to ascribe greater significance to the baptismal liturgy than we have in recent practice, but that Baptism and Eucharist are deeply complementary in their meaning and significance. The celebration of the rite in the presence of the assembled congregation also implies that the child is being incorporated into their life of corporate prayer. There can be no greater anomaly than to feel something has been achieved with the celebration of Baptism at a principal Sunday liturgy if the rite does not find its fulfillment in the giving of Communion to those who have been baptized. Similarly, it is an anomaly if, in the case of the Baptism of infants and small children, the newly baptized are not seen henceforth as integral members of that assembly. Each baptized person, adult or infant, brings into the community the particular gifts God gives to each one of us, gifts intended to bear fruit within the life of that community and ultimately for the good of our world. As the child grows and develops, those gifts are manifested, or often even drawn forth from the person as they seek to serve. In other words, it is not only that the child changes by being brought into the community of faith, but the community itself changes as the mystery of another believer's life unfolds in the context of the community.

Resistance to the full incorporation of children into the worshiping community is understandable. Their presence inevitably confronts the presuppositions about worship which have dominated liturgical practice. As adults, we tend to take for granted that liturgical worship will be very much tied to the Book of Common Prayer, though many visitors to an Episcopal Church have great difficulty finding their way through it. Parish priests have often commented to me that the BCP is not user-friendly. If this applies to visiting adults, it would apply all the more to children who could not read the book even if they had the strength to hold it.

This is not said to devalue the importance of the Book of Common Prayer in the history of Anglican worship and the significant role it has served as a sign of unity. But it is important to remember that a litur-

* We should remember that the idea that children were not appropriate communicants would have amazed and confused Christians of the first millennium, and would still be rejected by Eastern Orthodox Christians even today, since they have maintained the practice of infant Communion up to the present day.

gical celebration is far more than merely the words printed in the Prayer Book, just as a performance of a symphony by Beethoven is much more than the symbols printed on the pages of the score. The words like the notes are the point of departure for a living enactment engaged by active participants.

Similarly, a liturgical celebration is more than words, even the words of an inspired sermon. In recent years we have become more aware that a sermon is more than merely a sharing of information about God—it is a communication of the reality of God from one believer (the preacher) to a community of believers, in which the living Word is engaged not merely by the mind but by the heart, by the whole person. In preaching to congregations in which many children were present, I learned that what is required is a communication of self through stories from my own life and the lives of others in which the Gospel of Christ may be seen as active, and in which faith is nurtured and through which people are enabled to re-claim the presence of God's grace in our lives. In my experience, this type of preaching engages people of all ages, from childhood to old age; it is not merely a mental exercise, although the mind is also engaged.

Adult expectations also have tended to be shaped by a clergy-dominant model of celebration. Although the spirit of the 1979 BCP clearly envisions a more diverse model of liturgical leadership, some parishes still operate on a model in which the clergy, the choir and assisting ministers "do" the liturgy for the congregation. The architecture of most of our church buildings tends to reinforce this model. But the presence of children confronts these expectations. Even at an early age, children want to become involved in what is happening: they want to bring the bread and wine to the presider; they want, when they are able, to read from the Scripture—and they often read extraordinarily well. With children present, there is a kind of flow of spontaneity: one can never be sure exactly what will happen, and the presider must often go along with the unexpected.

Unfortunately, such a model can be difficult for people who have for years been accustomed to an almost absolute stability in what unfolds on Sunday morning. This model can be found also in the models of educa-tion which we have inherited especially from the practices of the nine-teenth century. The members of the congregation, like students at their desks, are all lined up in a row, and the presider, like the teacher, is the fo-cus of the action. Just as this model has been acknowledged as signifi-cantly deficient as an effective means of education, so also it must be judged as an ineffective model of liturgical celebration. It may be familiar in adult experience, but it generally betrays the nature of the liturgy as a multi-sensual act in which all the senses are involved, and not merely the eyes and ears. Children bring a gift for this type of liturgy into the assembly because they are multi-sensual by nature. In the past, the purpose of chil-dren's chapels, in which the furniture and appointments were all miniature versions of those in the adult space, was to prepare children for the time when they could behave well enough in the restricted space of the adult congregation to be able to join them for their model of worship.

The learning should be going in the opposite direction, and this is the gift which children can offer to the adult community. If we avoid the solution of modest adjustments to the adult model and engage the larger challenge of developing a new one appropriate to the whole worshiping community, including both children and the very elderly, not only will the unfolding of the liturgy necessarily change, but also the space in which we gather will need to be altered in order to serve the congregation by supporting a participatory model of corporate worship.

Children are profoundly sensitive to the attitudes which adults show toward them, often without the use of words. When parents wanted to bring their children to Jesus for a blessing, the disciples tried to stop them. It is possible to sentimentalize this passage in the gospel and to see it merely as a sweet Jesus taking little children into his arms. But the passage is far more radical and challenging than that. Jesus had taught the disciples that the Kingdom of God was breaking in upon the world now, and so the disciples seemed to think that in the face of such a momentous event, Jesus should not be bothered with such a trivial request. But the response of Jesus is one of indignation. Jesus is angry that the disciples have not understood his teaching on God's reign: "Do not hinder them, for to such as these belongs the Kingdom of God. Truly I say to you, whoever does not receive the Kingdom of God as a little child shall not enter in." (Mark 10:13–16) In their natural gifts of awe, trust, wonder, and thankfulness, children can reveal to us the imperative of a new heart and mind, of a new way into the life of grace, and of new models of corporate worship as we enter together into the cosmic dance as the children of God.

Louis Weil
Church Divinity School of the Pacific

Preface

In the early eighties, I tended bar for a living at one of the several neighborhood taverns in the Russian Hill area of San Francisco. The bartenders would gather after our two o'clock closing, for breakfast, or drinks, or both.

One night, one of the bartenders from across the street dropped in, grabbed me by the hand, and told me he had a surprise. Did I want to see it? Bill was an attorney by day, a blender of exotic drinks by night.

Well, yes. I did want to see it. Whatever it was, I was game.

We walked to the financial district, entered one of the bank buildings by its side door—Bill had a key, which impressed me—and descended several flights of stairs deep into the bowels of that building, which then fed into a central room from which ran several long cement corridors.

Catacombs in San Francisco. I'd never have guessed.

It was dark. Bill held my hand, or I should say, I gripped his.

One room, then another. A corridor veering at right angles. A succession of corridors, right turns, left turns, big rooms, small rooms. All concrete. Nothing to distinguish one from another. I wondered where I was, and I wondered if I would ever find my way back into the light.

Bill stopped from time to time, as though to get his bearings. Once we retraced our steps to make a different choice.

I sensed, rather than saw, the tension leave Bill's body, and felt a smile come across his face.

The hand that held mine pointed. Over there.

We walked to a corner of the room.

Bill released my hand, and I heard something scrape. A chair, maybe. A small table.

It was a piano bench and Bill sat, pulling me down alongside him.

In the pitch black of the underground—morning was probably breaking on the street—Bill began to play scales on a piano, orienting himself.

Then he played.

He played hymns. He played the hymns I had learned as a child. Hymns I'd not sung for perhaps fifteen years. "Holy, holy, holy!" "Eternal Father, strong to save." "Abide with me."

He played and we sang. I sang as though I had rehearsed the words as recently as that morning. Songs I'd ingested at such depth and such an early age that they'd never left me.

Memory awakened and stretched.

Tears coursed down my cheeks.

Tears of loneliness. Tears of such longing as to cause me pain. Tears of a deep and abiding hunger.

This dark windowless cement room in underground San Francisco became, for that moment, my church, the church I'd abandoned years before, not out of anger but from despair, a church that had nothing to do with me.

We sang in a timelessness of our own design and desire.

And finally, as we re-emerged into the morning light, and not by any means through the way we had entered, I wondered, what might it be like to come back.

Could I come back?

What might it have been like, I wondered, not to have left in the first place.

Acknowledgments

Louis Weil, who anchors us in our baptismal covenant; Kearney Riet-mann who turned a congregation on its head; Lynn Bauman for his many late nights formatting the manuscript; Philip Broyles, for his unwavering support and humor; Lanny Vincent, whose casual remark founded a web community; Bill Dols, the theologian of the project for his interfaith vision; Ward Bauman, for his modeling of authentic ministry; Cathy Roskam, who told me what I could and could not get away with; Nigel Renton, whose commas and word changes are evident throughout; Ruthie Pocock and Kay Nelson, who appear with the right stuff at the right moments; Joan Castagnone, my editor, whose willingness to uphold a vision has made this book possible. I thank you all.

Welcome to Worship

Beginnings: The Broad View

If you broaden your understanding of what it means to be the corporate body at worship, broaden it enough to include your community's children at worship with you, you will step onto an exhilarating, unpredictable, sometimes confusing path of a congregation in bloom, whose promise is the approach of the Kingdom of God.

There are those of you in every congregation who are saying, "Something is not quite right about worshiping in ways that segregate." This is your book.

This a book for the whole people of God, lay or ordained, officially titled or not, who are called to a ministry of inclusion.

Children know God. They experience the sacred in all kinds of ways and at a depth that often surprises adults.

In 1992, I was called to Holy Family Church in Half Moon Bay, California, to build a program of Children's Ministries. As you follow the story of our journey, remember that we had no clue as to what that program, faithfully undertaken, might mean for the worshiping community.

In the seven years I served Holy Family Church, the population of our children and youth increased from under ten to about a hundred-twenty.

The program we developed is very simple: it consists of weekly worship whose heart is Holy Communion. Sundays consist of a cracking open of the Word of God in a variety of ways: storytelling, art, drama, and music.

Sundays consist of the kind of education that is born of the experience of God's love made evident in the love of the community. Sundays consist of education and reflection.

Mission Congregation

Holy Family Episcopal Church is a mission congregation in the Diocese of California, and it is blessed with children. Lots of children.

Mission churches and children have a lot in common, and it has to do with their capacity to create and re-create and be re-created. Children and missions reflect the same heady excitement of things becoming...and it's a becoming out of the emptiness.

Holy Family is a mission church, and within that status many things are possible. Mission churches, if they are to stay afloat, have to be clever and bold and daring. Mission churches live at the intersection of invention and pragmatism.

But there's more.

Mission congregations serve the church as the seat of our memory, that moment of creation, in which all things that can be imagined are possible. Mission congregations call us to remember a time when we could build kingdoms with a block of wood and a piece of string and a rubber band.

In that sense, mission congregations can be the church's gift to itself, the standard-bearers of its vision, living and serving, by definition, at the edges.

Their season is Advent, a time of deep scrutiny and the heady excitement of things becoming out of the emptiness.

Whatever we talk about, in terms of program for change—whether it's adult ministries or children's ministries, or jail ministries, or hospital ministries—it has to proceed out of that place. Out of the void, the emptiness.

My purpose here is to reveal our children's program in this light. I want to show you what it is that we've developed, and how we've developed it, beginning at the God-centered place of emptiness—the only place where it makes sense to speak of re-creation and transformation.

You have heard it said, "The children are the future."

Who is saying that? Not the children. Ask a child if she's the future. If she could even grab hold of the question, which I doubt, she'll tell you that she's the moment. She's the now. Or, more to the point, she's hungry. And to appreciate and address her hunger is to turn the church upside down.

Adults are the ones who talk about children as the future. It seems to me that within that statement, far more is said than intended.

Children are our future, so we better make sure they stay in the church. Or at least we better make sure that they come back. Children are our future so we'll develop programs that are child-friendly.

It's very seductive.

The program we developed is very simple: it consists of weekly worship whose heart is Holy Communion.

You have heard it said, "The children are the future." Who is saying that? Not the children. Ask a child if she's the future. If she can even grab hold of the question, which I doubt, she'll tell you that she's the moment. She's the now. Or more to the point, she's hungry.

Evolution and Renewal

Our churches have done spiritual damage, and continue to do so, not by design, but by inattentiveness, perhaps, or fear, or by our inclination to allow our liturgies to go unexamined. We opt for the familiar, for the convenient.

We often speak to one another about the need for congregational change and revitalization, and we are often correct. But most of us try to apply the solutions before we do the work of spiritual examination. We embark on a "try these shoes" frenzy and as we try and then quickly discard, our discouragement grows.

Although this book is about the practical applications of the work of renewal as it has unfolded in one small congregation, the work is far broader. The people of Holy Family Church discovered that their theology of community, which came to be expressed in liturgy, spilled over into every aspect of their congregational life.

This will be true as well for your congregation. You will begin to function as a community, make decisions as a community, expand your understanding of congregational ministry.

But always remember that what works for one congregation may not work in another. What works for that congregation today will evolve further tomorrow. This book is built around the centrality of change, in our lives and in our liturgies, using one community's children as the centerpiece.

Children at Worship is built upon principles of liturgical evolution. Understood properly, our liturgies are designed to reflect, to respond to and to deepen the spirituality of the worshipping congregations. By definition, then, liturgies must evolve. Can we not learn to embrace the principles of evolution as necessary and highly desirable?

The difficulty in the writing of this book lies in its fundamental premise: the liturgies of a community of faith are designed both to express and to deepen the spiritual work of the congregation. In order to do that, liturgies must evolve even as the spirit deepens, or they become a tight skeleton around the body, like the exoskeleton of a lobster.

Evolving liturgies, by definition, are difficult to delineate within the bounds of a book.

Consider the process of this manuscript over a six-month period. A draft was sent out to selected readers, whose task it was to comment on the content.

Readers' critiques came in over the summer, and by early fall, I had arranged six weeks of sabbatical time to revise, format, and submit the manuscript for publication.

Two weeks prior to my departure, however, I began to hear rumblings. Nothing major. Just those clues that it's time to take another step. Just as I believed that this manuscript was ready to go, I began to hear the still-inarticulate voices of people expressing a hunger to go deeper.

It is important to say this, because the liturgical work of a congregation is never finished. We speak of the forms of worship as though they were gods. Our liturgical churches are masters at this.

Yet, even as I offer this book as the best of our efforts to date, we are constantly called ever deeper into the corporate expression of praise and adoration that belongs only to God. The forms and decisions offered here were already changing as I wrote this book and continue to change as you read it.

Children at Worship: Congregations in Bloom

Realizing the fluid nature of this process, the question quickly became, "How do we continue and foster this conversation after the book is published? With that question, an idea was formed, and with the idea, an organization.

Children at Worship: Congregations in Bloom is a non-profit, tax-exempt, grassroots association of lay and ordained ministers of churches and other organizations who are committed to the fundamental questions of community.

We are teachers of a radical sort, and we teach congregations and clusters of congregations the precepts and strategies of full inclusion in our worship communities. We are priests, musicians, artists, preachers, laborers, architects, administrators, and dreamers.

We believe we pay a grievous price for a single voice lost. We know the value of the voices and perspectives of our children and youth. Our hearts beat with the urgent need to transform our traditional and often exclusive forms of worship into structures which engage whole communities. We are committed to the enfranchisement, empowerment, and full participation of everyone, particularly children, and all those who have remained at the edges of our churches.

Consider us as your resource center for inclusive and engaging worship. Make use of our interactive website:

www.childrenatworship.org
Children at Worship: Congregations in Bloom
info@childrenatworship.org (e-mail)

Use This Book

This is a book of many voices: voices of children; voices of their parents; voices of lay and ordained educators; voices that cross denominations and speak from outside the Christian faith. This book carries the voices of tradition; the voices of the prophets and theologians; the voices of the artists. Mostly this is the collective voice of the child in all of us.

If you don't yet recognize your own voice in these chapters, then add it; speak it. There is a dream at work here, and it is the dream of conversion. There are congregations, educators, and people of faith in every pocket of the world who understand and commit to the renewal of our faith. These are the voices that belong in this book and those to follow.

While I use many words and pictures from the children of Holy Family, the names are fictitious unless attached to specific poetry or art.

This Book is a Teaching Text

People in congregations often speak to me of their isolation, their lack of support. Fear drives this sense of aloneness, I think. God hasn't given us the gifts of prophecy and discernment and vision only to allow them to shrivel. There are fellow pilgrims in your communities. Your task is to identify them.

Use this book to teach one another. Use it to convert one another. Use it to build a congregational core grounded in the principles contained here: principles of full inclusion; of the priesthood of all believers; mutual ministry; principles of discernment. Make sure that these principles form the basis of the work of discernment and vision. Use this book to challenge your clergy. Use it to paint a new dream. Use it as a tool for the revitalization of your faith community. Use it to carry this conversation outside the borders of your own denominations.

I have written this book from three perspectives; each is woven into each chapter.

First, I write as a leader and designer of worship. For those of you who do what I do, lay or ordained, my hope is to touch on the joys and difficulties, the hopes and promises of the kind of work that we do, weekly, seasonally, year in, year out.

Second, I write from the experience and the stories of Holy Family Church. And here is my hope—as more and more of us are drawn into the conversation, the "we" will expand to include the experiences, stories and struggles from congregations across denominations and across the borders of faiths. The voice of "we the people of God" cannot help but grow if we use this book as the beginning of our discussions.

Third, my hope is to carry a theological thread throughout each chapter. It not only matters what we do and how we do it, but why.

In the sidebars of each chapter, you will find questions for reflection. As you use these and others you might develop, remember that these conversations need to happen congregation-wide. Choose participants for the breadth of their opinions. Let the conversations be difficult.

Most of us in faith families are hungry. Most of us want the same food. We let ourselves be deterred by fear, anxiety, tradition, and our own early church experiences.

Design conversations in an informal setting, perhaps around a meal. Include children and youth. This is critical. Get in the habit of saying to yourselves, "Never again may we have a conversation about our congregational vision that does not include our young people."

The Children's Charter

At its convention in 1997, the Episcopal Church adopted the Children's Charter for the Church. This document calls the people of God in three ways: to the nurture of children; to minister to children; and to discern and raise up the ministries of children.

The principles, applications, suggestions, anecdotes and resources contained in this book derive from the goals and purposes set forth in the Children's Charter.

In particular, this book is concerned with the ministries of children. How does a faith community live into its vocation of the ministry of all the baptized?

The Children's Charter reads, in part, "The Church is called: to receive children's special gifts as signs of the Reign of God; to foster community beyond family, in which children, youth and adults know each other by name, minister to each other, and are partners together in serving Christ in the world; to take their place in the life, worship and governance of the church."

Children belong in church. They belong in the regular worship life of their faith community. And they need to be honored and recognized as fully participatory partners in the decision making of the body.

The Children's Charter is reprinted in Appendix A.

Children Belong in Church

By virtue of the covenant we make or the covenant that is made on our behalf at our Baptism, children belong in church. Our Baptism compels us to understand even the "least of these" as fully participating members of the eucharistic community. What that means is that they are integral to the regular worship of the congregation.

But to understand the theology of inclusion is only one step in the process of discovery. For it is not until communities have reconfigured their regular worship in such a way as to allow for the participation and engagement of their children, that they will even begin to understand the transformative power of this decision. Children belong in church, and every time a community opts for the inclusion of its children, that conviction will sink ever deeper

In Closing

As the fruits of our work come to you in the form of this book, an adaptation of a Benedictine prayer floats through my mind:

I ask you to pray for my conversion, as I continue to pray for yours.

Shalom.

Let the Children Come to Me

Chapter Two

Harriet and I

Though neither of us knew it at the time, my childhood friend Harriet taught me a lesson I will never forget.

She used to take me into the woods in the early spring. We'd go belly down into the snow-soaked leaves of maple and oak, and we'd wait.

Harriet was better at it than I.

"What are we waiting for this time?" I'd ask her.

"Sh-h-h. I don't know yet."

And with that admission my spirits would sink. It was likely we'd be there a long time.

"Are you sure you don't know?"

"I won't know until I see it."

"Oh."

And then, there it would be, in front of our eyes. Maybe just sitting there for the longest time before we could see it. Before we could do whatever it was that was required of us—slow ourselves down, be silent, pay attention, wait, trust.

Maybe the young shoot of a Western Pennsylvania narcissus or a daffodil. Maybe a sluggish beetle coming to life on a warm March afternoon. Or a spider crawling up a new blade of grass. A mushroom. A puff ball. Or a robin, bringing a flash of color to the still-drab woods.

"Just wait," Harriet would tell me.

We were never disappointed. Never.

And the subjects of our discovery became our teachers. They instructed us in God. Instructed us in God's world. Our teachers made us laugh. A fuzzy orange caterpillar swimming over pine needles and soggy maple leaves on his way to some clandestine and mysterious ritual, deep into the heart of the forest. Our teachers would have us hold our breaths in the face of their splendor. An eight-point buck rubbing his vel-

Stories

- Never underestimate the power of personal stories.
- Personal stories draw children into any discussion about God.
- Personal stories help children expand their understanding of the sacred.

vet antlers against an ancient and gnarled apple tree. They'd have us run away. A Pennsylvania black snake, gentle as she was, could do it every time.

We lived in our own timelessness, Harriet and I. Not even our stomachs betrayed us.

The world in which Harriet and I found ourselves was limitless in its possibilities. Maybe it was an acre beneath our knees and our hands and our bellies, maybe a hundred acres. It didn't matter. We were explorers and full participants in the world of tall grasses, bugs, mud, water, trees, rocks, and the creatures under the rocks. Skunks and opossums and bobtail cats. Nothing was out of bounds. No shout of joy or surprise, no scream, no laughter, no ceiling of any kind did we put on our discovery.

"Just wait," Harriet would tell me. "We'll know it when we see it."

Surprise

The spirits of children are like that, surprise after surprise, springing up from their inexhaustible soil.

Teaching. Cajoling. Inspiring. Transforming.

"Just wait," Harriet would tell me. "We'll know it when we see it."

One Sunday in Lent, I said to the children of Holy Family Church, "There's a special day coming. Who can tell me what it is?"

"Easter!"

"What about Easter?"

"Easter bunnies!"

"Easter eggs!"

"Easter baskets with lots of jellybeans!"

And then I got lucky.

"Jesus!!!"

Easter Bunnies and Easter eggs, jelly beans and Jesus. It's as good a theology as any we come by. Because in those things are contained all of life...life in all its paradox. Its exhilaration and its terror. Its death and rebirth. The losses. The surprises. The sweetness and the laughter, the joys, the sorrows.

And always the promise. The bittersweet promise of change and transformation.

A five-year-old named John explained to me that Jesus didn't die from being nailed to the cross. He died from a heart attack.

Nicole disagreed. "It was the nails," she said. "There was poison in the nails."

Grown-ups often get squirmy listening to these things. Especially parents. "O my God, my child said the wrong thing. I'm a terrible parent. Everybody's going to know it. "

Or else we say, "How cute."

But the idea of Jesus dying from a heart attack is neither wrong nor cute. John's father had had a heart attack. And everything this child knew about pain and death and loss and fear was set within the

- Children learn by what they see, hear, taste, touch, and smell.
- Sensory learning is integral to the spiritual development of children.
- The goal is to provide a rich sensory experience for the educational context.

context of that heart attack. It made great sense to talk of the pain and death and loss of Jesus in terms of a heart attack.

And the poison nails? Nicole told me that nails weren't bad in themselves. There were nails in the walls of her house and nails in her swing set. It wasn't the nails that were bad; it was the poison in them.

Nicole won't talk to you about sin and she won't talk to you about the evil that we do to one another. But she'll talk at great length about poison. The poison in the nails that killed Jesus.

The world of children is limitless in its possibilities, a world like Harriet and I shared. It is a world in which metaphor is reality. A world not constrained by the boundaries we have come to know as adults. Perhaps in that world we are closer to the Kingdom. That's a scary thought.

Accommodating Children

We try to convince ourselves that the accommodation of children doesn't really require a change in the patterns of the adult worshiping congregation.

That's correct, by the way. The accommodation of children does not have to change much of anything.

If we do a children's story or have youthful acolytes or invite the children into the procession or teach them to sing an offertory hymn... we console ourselves that a little disorganization is a small price to pay for the continuity of our worship.

When we think about children and liturgy, we use words like "hospitality" and "welcoming" and "accommodating." These are good words, friendly words, useful words. But the problem is, when we use them in reference to members of our own congregations, we create a division by definition. We and they. We are welcoming them. We are providing hospitality for them. We belong. They are the visitors.

It's a dangerous assumption, in my opinion, and one which is all too common.

I loved the church of my childhood. White clapboard outside, cool inside and redolent with the smells of brass polish and furniture oil mixed with the faintest hint of Lysol.

But we kids weren't in the big church for long. We were moved quickly to the old house down the street, where we spent most of our time in table desks, desks in rows and columns with square corners, desks so close to the ground you could scoot them about with your knees. "Carol Fairless, if you cut off Robin Roberts's head with an axe... would that be a sin?"

Mr. Hackett had eighty of us in Sunday school, and he could keep our attention.

He shouted those words at me as though I'd actually done that heinous deed. I nodded, of course, and allowed as how I thought that would probably be a sin. I have wonderful warm memories of that giant of a man who cared enough about kids to go to the mat with us Sunday after Sunday.

But I'd rather have been in church.

"Whenever the air is clear and pure, the sun must infuse itself into the air and cannot keep from doing so. In the same way, whenever and wherever God finds you empty, God must act and infuse himself into you."

Meister Eckhart

I felt safe in the church. I belonged. I learned the hymns. I learned the prayers, albeit some of them imperfectly.

When one year my big sister Nancy was chosen to be the Virgin Mary in the Christmas pageant, I shouted out loud, "When Nancy shall come to judge the quick and the dead." I was very proud.

The next year an eighth grader named Sandy was chosen, and I relearned the Creed. "When Sandy shall come to judge…"

I loved the church and yet…my brother Ben was an acolyte. Puck was an acolyte. Pete was an acolyte. George, Tom, and David were acolytes. John was an acolyte. Tim was an acolyte.

I was not an acolyte.

I suffered Sunday after Sunday. I wanted to be an acolyte. I knew I could light and extinguish those candles on the very first try. I knew I could carry the cross and not drop it. But I wasn't allowed.

Still…I loved the church.

But I left it. I left it for nearly twenty years. Those were formative years, late adolescence and early adulthood. They were the years of first apartments, first jobs, and first loves. They were the years of quick decisions and dangerous times and I had no community of support, no extended family to foster my spiritual development. I justified my withdrawal in all kinds of ways. Church didn't have meaning for me. It was boring. I was always a visitor, never at home.

Then one day I came back. I didn't come back for the Scripture. I didn't come back for the preaching. I didn't even come back for the fellowship or the good works.

I came back because I remembered the smell of brass polish and furniture wax. I came back because I walked by a church one Sunday and remembered the words of the hymn they were singing. I came back because it was the season of Advent and my color was purple.

I came back because I had been safe there, once upon a time, and maybe I could find something like that again.

What might it be like to not leave, I wonder? Is leaving a given? Or is it just possible that the church could become what its own vision insists—a place of celebration and reflection and full participation—a shared meal for all who dare come. I talked with my friend Cathy not long ago, who told me that the model for her priesthood was her mother, a woman who never turned a single person away from her table.

A New Voice

Might we allow ourselves to hear a new voice? The voice of those who recognize that "accommodation" is not the vision.

Our congregation was transformed by such a voice.

One night, deep in the heart of a series of conversations around the possibility of adding a family worship service to the Sunday schedule, this voice cried out, "If we're still insisting on separating the children from the adults for the bulk of the service, then the children should worship in the sanctuary and let the adults move to the classrooms."

It wasn't a particularly angry voice, just a voice frustrated with the tenor of our conversations, which, admittedly was timid.

For Reflection:
- How is the word "hospitality" divisive when it's applied to members of your own community?
- When you first joined your present congregation, how did you come to participate in its common life?

For Reflection:
- When have you heard the prophet's voice in your own congregation?
- How have you responded?

Worship patterns are powerful things.

With that lone voice I felt as though I were trying to cling to the stem of a glass that had just shattered. Like many people, I was reluctant to follow the path that opened to me.

We see this in every revolution, I think. When the voice of the prophet steps across the line that distinguishes accommodation from transformation.

Mine is not the voice of the prophet. The prophetic voice comes from the congregation, and that's a very good thing.

Ask yourselves this question: "What happens when we dare assume that children have the same claim on the space, ritual, style, and content of worship as do adults?" It's a subversive question.

The people of Holy Family Church made the decision to work from that assumption. If you do the same, it will be life-changing for your congregations. And who knows...it may even release the child in each of us!

Our children have the identical claim on the space, ritual, style and content of worship as adults. It's a dangerous assumption, but it happens to be the right one.

At Holy Family, we didn't come to articulate that vision at the beginning. In fact, we tripped over it only when we turned the corner into our third year.

Ours was an evolutionary process. Our greatest leaps were in direct response to the voices of our children.

Every time we met, without fail, the children of Holy Family told us, sometimes in words, other times in tasks, or outreach, or art, where they were on their spiritual journey and what they needed. The children always tell us, but do we always listen?

Listening is a hard way to be with someone. Too hard, it would seem. The power that derives from listening isn't a culturally acceptable kind of power, or even recognizable as power. We don't want to listen. Listening goes against our nature. We want to *do* something—fix it, and build it up. Build up ourselves as clever counselors. Listening is an undoing. It's a surrender of self. A surrender of expertise. A surrender into Other.

Listening is the power of letting go, of washing away assumptions and preconceived ideas. Listening is a cleansing. It's the power of creating space for the Other.

It's our surrender into emptiness.

We learned to listen to our children, and it was hard fought, not only for the adults, but the children as well.

We practiced listening. We practiced it with an intentionality that transcended our expertise, which was a very good thing.

Holy Family Church has developed a program which is celebrated in the Diocese of California, celebrated in the community, and celebrated in the broader church.

I celebrate it every day, because it has changed my life.

One day I was painting the fingernails of a three-year-old. I was sure I had better things to do. But she looked at me and smiled a smile that tripled the size of my heart. "God loves this color," she told me.

"How do you know?"

What happens when we dare assume that children have an identical claim on the space, ritual, style and content of worship as do adults?

One day I was painting the fingernails of a three-year-old. I was sure I had better things to do. But she looked at me and smiled a smile that tripled the size of my heart.
"God loves this color," she told me.
"How do you know?"
"Because it's the color of fire."

See Eric Law's *The Gift of Diversity* for his thoughts about Pentecost of the ear, versus Pentecost of the tongue.

"Because it's the color of fire."

If you're not listening, you miss it.

Listening.

Listening is the first step. And the second is understanding wisdom in a new way.

Wisdom.

Wisdom often translates to tradition.

But they are not the same things. Tradition, as valuable as it may be, masquerades as wisdom. But wisdom does not carry with it any coercive application. We not only hold wisdom with an open hand, but we offer her as an open gesture.

So. If the wisdom is not "children are the future," then the question becomes, "What are our children?"

Our children are the ones who carry the most compelling, unadorned, intense, immediate, intimate relationship with all that is holy and sacred.

Our children understand the joy and the pain of all God's creatures...human creatures, creatures of the sea, of the land, of the air.

Our children are the world's healers.

Our children know the integrity of things.

Our children are empty... and hungry for God.

Share the Good News

Chapter Three

The teaching and preaching vocation of the Christian church has endured throughout the centuries. *Didache* and *Kerygma* are their formal names. In our relatively recent history, we have separated these functions, particularly with regard to children. We preach in the church and we teach in the classroom.

Although we offer a Sunday opportunity for adult education, and call that Sunday school as well, for the most part, when we speak of Sunday school, we mean children segregated, to some degree or other, from the worship community.

As a seminarian, Sunday school was described to me in this way: "A microcosm of congregational life." I had already spent a good part of my adult life relegated to some undercroft in the bowels of the church, or spread out on a floor with basketball lines, the whole of which smelled like old socks.

Closer to the truth was that I'd worked with enough "cotton ball Jesus" exercises to buy me many indulgences. I'd heard enough bad children's sermons in my life, delivered in the falsettos of adults who thought that such tones somehow served to capture a child's attention.

I did not realize at the time that my entire grasp of what Sunday mornings mean, was about to undergo a radical transformation.

Fear

People describe their fears and anxieties around preaching and teaching with children in various ways.

"I don't know how to do it."

"I'm afraid."

"I'm inadequate."

Some of this fear derives from confusion, I think. We aren't quite sure about the task, which is, I believe, to crack open like a

For Reflection:
- Take a moment with pen and paper to write down your assumptions regarding preaching with children.
- What are your assumptions about children's sermons?
- Do you have assumptions about the need to sanitize Scripture?

When a child tells you that a flower is going to die whether or not it is connected to the vine, that child has not ruined your sermon; that child has opened up a conversational opportunity about the quality of life lived in God.

For Reflection:

When a child's words evoke laughter from the congregation, how do we make this a rich experience for that child, rather than an embarrassing one?

seed is cracked open, the Living Word of God. In this way, it is a mutual ministry, not a didactic one.

A colleague preaches a children's sermon one Sunday a month. He gathers the children to sit on the floor at the foot of the chancel step. He stands at the top, his knees at eye level. He takes out all the big words from the scriptural story; he cleans it up by removing what he calls the controversial parts; he changes the tenor of his voice altogether. He preaches to the children, but he makes eye contact with the adults seated in the congregation. He preaches, literally, over their heads. The children won't tell you about the sermon, but they can give a pretty good account of the state of his pants at the knees.

A seminarian tells me she doesn't want to preach to children because she's afraid. As we explore this further, she tells me it's because children always ruin the point of her sermons. Give me an example, I ask her, and she tells me this story:

"I preached once to children, and the gospel was the 'I am the vine; you are the branches' discourse from the Gospel of John. I brought in a rose bush and referred to it as I read the story. I was trying to make the point about how we, as branches, live connected to Jesus.

"But—and I ripped a stem from the main trunk, very dramatically—if we tear this branch from the vine, what will happen to the flower?

"They all knew. It'll die. But there was one child in the back with his hand up. I had a feeling about this child, and I deliberately ignored him, hoping he'd get distracted and put his hand down.

"He didn't.

"I called on him, and he told all of us, in a very loud voice, that the flower is going to die anyway, even if it stays on the vine.

"He was right, of course, and everybody laughed, at my discomfort, no doubt, because he ruined the story."

But that child didn't ruin the story. He merely pointed out what all of us know and don't like to admit. We are going to die, one way or another. One moment or the next.

The gift that this particular child gave the congregation was an opportunity to reflect on the quality of life lived in God.

In terms of the Children's Charter, this is an instance of the power of a child's ministry to the congregation.

Comfortable or uncomfortable, I can promise you one thing. If I can be taught, by the children I serve, to stand with them in mutual discovery and celebration of the wonders of God, you can too. Use the ideas in this chapter, and let them stimulate your own godly conversations with the children of your congregation.

Evangelism Refocused: Children Thrive on Discovery

Maybe we don't all love to preach and teach with children, but not preaching and not teaching is not an option.

The four Gospels give us no shortage of ways in which to understand our charge to evangelize. Matthew's Gospel, perhaps the most familiar, says, "Go and make disciples of all nations, baptizing them in the name of the Father and of the Son and of the Holy

Spirit," a charge which seems to have justified just about every kind of behavior imaginable from the likes of street preachers and television evangelists, to your everyday common clergy-in-the-pulpit.

Think of it this way. To make disciples is dangerous language. A colleague says to me, "My job is to make converts, the more the better."

To make disciples, I believe, is to thwart a process of discovery.

Neither was it Jesus' way of converting. Jesus asked questions; he invited people into conversations. The woman at the well was invited into a process of godly discovery. Peter, at Caesarea Philippi, was invited into a process of godly discovery. Mary at Bethany was invited into a process of godly discovery.

Children thrive on discovery. It's how they learn, grow, deepen, dare. To stunt that process is to stunt their growth.

We have taught them Jesus much like we teach them their grammar or their multiplication tables. It's a debilitating process, and I believe it thwarts spiritual development for years. Adults say, "What am I supposed to believe to belong to your church?" Or, "What am I supposed to believe about Jesus?" Or, "Did Jesus really turn water into wine?" They are speaking from the theological framework of a six-year-old.

We must ask ourselves if we need to rethink some things.

It seems to me that another approach might serve better the call to evangelize. Perhaps our charge is to offer a framework for discipleship, or perhaps to support the discovery of discipleship.

It is not my job, or yours, as parent, as teacher or as clergy, to make people into anything. I wonder if we might investigate the making of disciples from another perspective. Consider, for example, the account recorded in the Gospel of Mark (16:15). Jesus charges his disciples to preach the Good News to all creation.

Preach the Good News to all creation. What might that mean if we were to take this charge seriously? Clearly we are called to preach to adults. Children, too. But what else? Are we to preach to the earth? The ocean? The sky?

How would you preach the Good News to, say, a tree?

Preaching to a Barren Fig Tree

What Good News would you impart to the fig tree in Chapter Thirteen of Luke's Gospel, a tree which refused to bear fruit for three years?

It seems to me that preaching to a barren fig tree would require some listening. Preaching to a fig tree would require that you look closely...at the soil, at the sun, at the season. Preaching to a fig tree would require that you get your hands dirty, digging down to determine the level of water. Preaching to a fig tree would require that you pay attention.

Only then might you be able to respond with your perspective. You might bring the Good News in terms of the Living Water. Or bring the Good News in terms of the necessity of pruning. Or perhaps the kind of food that could assuage its hunger.

Not teaching and not preaching is not an option.

For Reflection:

- How might you address the problem of a reluctant, non-bearing fruit tree?
- Are there any parallels among the relationships of your life?

15

Mark's understanding of evangelism, I believe, has more to do with an exchange of Good News than its didactic proclamation.

For Reflection:

- Practice listening to the children of your congregation.
- What Good News are they wanting to share with you?

Conversely, if this fig tree were a healthy, productive, fruit bearing tree, perhaps this tree would be bringing the Good News to us. There is this Living Water, if only you knew. There is food, abundant food, for your hunger, if only you knew. My seed was planted in the richest of soils, if only you knew.

How much we could learn from a fig tree! The fig tree already knows everything it needs to know about God.

Mark's understanding of evangelism, I believe, has more to do with an exchange of the Good News than it does the proclamation of it.

An exchange is what's required of us if we heed Mark's charge to bring the Good News to the whole of creation. An exchange is what's required of us with regard to preaching with children, an exchange of Good News. Children already know the Good News. In that sense, it is not even "news" to them.

There's a story that floats around congregations, and it goes like this.

Emma was four when her sister was born, and she was anxious to spend some time with her.

"Alone," she insisted to her mother. "You need to leave us alone. Please."

Her mother did, after the fashion of mothers who listen at the door, and she heard Emma whisper to her sister, "Can you remind me how it is with God? Because I'm already beginning to forget."

Emma's fear and experience is the same for all of us. The readiness and wonder to engage the mystery is educated out of us, and from a young age.

Children *know* the Good News of God already, and they continue to discover it, intensely, and passionately. Their's is a steep learning curve. And they want to share it.

Children give adults who listen a wild, uncontainable, flyaway, spillover jumble of God's Good News.

Adults, sadly, are in the habit of diminishing, or even ignoring all that, for the sake of curriculum, doctrine, order, and perhaps even convenience.

If we are already explaining to our children what the Good News means before we even hear them tell it, then we are doing damage. Adults need first to listen, and then to be about the work of removing obstacles, sometimes including ourselves, to our children's spiritual growth and expression.

We can make a shift from the arrogance of "preaching to" to the mutuality of exchange. What we familiarly call evangelism becomes a process of mutual discovery, mutual enrichment.

Getting Started

The first step in incorporating children into worship is to make decisions about the form and content of worship. One piece of worship I dare say all denominations hold in common is the Liturgy of the Word, that is, the telling of the biblical story.

Many denominations read Scripture from the Hebrew Scriptures (Old Testament), the Epistles (New Testament), and from the

Gospels (New Testament). What kinds of decisions might we make about the storytelling? What story will it be? A creation story? A story with a theme? A story about Jesus? A Parable? Passion narrative?

The first decision might center on the choice of story. Which of the possibilities lend themselves to powerful and dramatic storytelling ?

Who is to tell the story? Chances are there are gifted storytellers of all ages in your congregations. Some, perhaps, read exceedingly well. Others may have a gift in biblical narrative, some in biblical drama. Some may write well, while others speak.

Don't assume that the function of *kerygma* belongs solely to the priest. Not all clergy are gifted storytellers.

Look around you. Pay attention. Pay particular attention to the narrative and dramatic gifts of youth and older children. Let it be known that your congregation is looking to build up a body of storytellers.

Where are the children to sit? Do they sit together, and up front? Do they sit with their families? Sometimes one place, sometimes another?

The question of seating depends on what you intend to do.

How do you want them to participate in the joy and wonder and discovery of the storytelling...today? Although there are many occasions when you might ask the children to remain seated with their parents, if it's full participation that you are seeking, then bring them forward, and know full well that their energy will infect one another. Know also that children can hear and learn under the most extraordinary of circumstances.

This brings us to the next question: how is the story to be told? Straight biblical narrative? Drama? Write your own play? Engage children and adults in interactive conversation? Invite the participation of the entire congregation.

If there is a sermon, at what point will it be preached? If young children and youth are present, then a sermon must be developed with them in mind. Don't preach long! Don't assume that just because children are sitting still they are paying attention. It is a fair bet that any sermon designed with clarity enough so that a child can understand it will be heard as well by the adults in the way they need to hear it.

At Holy Family Church, I would often preach an adult sermon following Communion. The children could stay, if they wished, or exit to the art rooms. But they knew that it was adult time, and if they chose to stay, there were adult expectations upon them.

These are decisions that each congregation needs to make for itself, based on the needs and composition of the worshiping community.

Don't hesitate to make use of the breadth and depth of children's literature available commercially. The Very Reverend Alan Jones, Dean of Grace Cathedral in San Francisco, on many occasions makes the claim that much of contemporary literature has a theological foundation that is not only as sound, but far more so than many of the books which make a claim to theology. There are myriad ways and styles of storytelling. It behooves congregations, I think, to avail themselves of a variety. Think in terms of a storytelling stew.

Attentiveness

Another concern, of course, is the noise factor. How do you teach children the art of attentiveness? I have been in conversation recently with a woman whose congregation has opened up its worship to children of the neighborhood, most of whom have never been in church.

"They come with or without their parents," she told me. "Mostly without. It's as though they've never sat still in their lives. What do we do?"

Teach them. Don't assume that they know what is expected of them. Children in church is as new to the children as to any of the adults.

Practice periods of attentiveness. I don't say "periods of silence"; I say "attentiveness."

Introduce visual or aural symbols that call the congregation to attentiveness.

A bowl bell works very well

Holy Family Church has a large brass bell bowl in the sanctuary, and it is used primarily as a call to attentiveness.

At first it was just that, but the use of the bowl has evolved in several ways. Its sound is a call to prayer, and in particular, silent prayer. Within the resonance of that bowl can be heard the voice of God in its many and varied forms. It's a call to story. The bell bowl is struck; the storyteller puts on her/his story cloak, and the children are ready to engage in the Good News.

Make a Storyteller's Cloak

Attune yourselves to opportunities which help children be attentive. One such opportunity is the building of a Storyteller's Cloak. It's something any congregation can do.

Here's how Holy Family Church did it.

Several of our storytellers wrote on flash cards the titles of biblical stories that our children had heard over the past couple years: Jesus raises Lazarus from the dead; the creation story; Moses brings the Law to the people; the golden calf; Jesus heals a man who was born blind; Jesus eats with prostitutes and tax collectors; Mary wipes the feet of Jesus with costly perfume.

We filled a paper sack with dozens of stories, and each week at story time, passed the sack to the children.

A child drew out "Mary sits at the feet of Jesus while Martha makes dinner in the kitchen." We told that story, all of us together. The children remembered wonderful things. Martha wanted some help in the kitchen. She sounds like my mom. She didn't want Mary to have a good time. Jesus let Mary stay where she wanted to stay. They spoke candidly about their feelings. The adult "Martha's" of the congregation identified themselves.

We passed the sack another time, and a child drew out "Moses hears the Voice of God from a burning bush." We then told that story, again, collaboratively.

A Storyteller's Cloak: Our storyteller's cloak is stitched from the fabric paintings of children who are intent on telling the biblical story.

Where was Moses? He was out with his sheep. What did he see? He saw a bush that was on fire. There was something odd about this bush. Can you tell me what that might have been? It was on fire, but it didn't burn up. Who spoke to Moses? God! Do you remember what God said? God told him to take off his shoes. Why, I wonder, would God tell Moses that? You can hear the wheels turning in the silence that follows. They're stumped.

"To give his shoes a break!"

The storyteller reminds them that Moses was on holy ground.

We shared stories for eight Sundays, four or five stories at a time. Each week, I told the children that I would like them to paint these stories on fabric squares. That we were going to put the squares together into a Storyteller's Cloak.

What's that?

You'll see.

One of the parents of the church took the squares and sewed them into a piece of brilliant blue fabric, and lined it inside with raw silk.

On that cloak itself are the pictorial representations of the stories of Hebrew Scriptures and the stories of the New Testament: Joseph and his coat of many colors; Jacob's ladder; Noah's ark; the crossing of the Dead Sea. The experience of Mary and Joseph as they sought refuge in Bethlehem is depicted by a Motel 8 with a "No Vacancy" sign out front. There is scene in which four men lower a pallet through the roof of a house. A mustard seed. A pearl of great value. A field of weeds and wheat. Jesus condemned. Jesus crucified. Jesus comes alive. Jesus on the road to Emmaus.

The entire effect is both elegant and powerful.

Picture this ritual. The bowl bell is struck. The congregation is called into attentiveness. The storyteller puts on the cloak. The children know this is the moment to hear the Word of God.

With children present, this is the moment that allows the intersection of proclamation and teaching, where *Kerygma* meets *Didache*.

In the sections which follow are examples and commentary of biblical stories and a sampling of commercial children's books which Holy Family Church has used over the years to broaden and deepen its community's relationship to God. My hope is that you will use these to crack open the many and rich resources that already exist in your own congregations.

As I set forth various storytelling styles and techniques, I will address some of the "nuts and bolts" questions as well.

Contemporary Literature as Biblical Adjunct

Helme Heine's *The Pearl* is a wonderful way to put a ironic twist to the parable of the pearl of great value (Mt 13:46). Beaver finds a freshwater pearl mussel, and in his obsession to guard the pearl within, he manages to alienate all his friends, destroy his dam, flood the fields, and set fire to the forest. But it's all a dream. When he wakes from this nightmare, Beaver heaves the freshwater pearl mussel back into the lake and spends a great deal of time checking in with his friends.

David Weisner's *Tuesday* is a powerful way to share the story of the plagues on Pharaoh's house and land. Using only pictures, it captures the horrors of the time in a whimsical way.

Spend time in the children's section of your book stores. Read catalogues. Start collecting. When you discover a book for children that can break open the scriptural story, grab it. Pay particular attention to good art.

The Biblical Story

Tell the Bible stories, and don't shy away from the Hebrew Scriptures. A friend once told me, with great dramatic passion, "The God of the Old Testament is no God of mine." She was referring to the Jacob and Esau story, saying that it wasn't fair that Jacob stole his brother's blessing and then became the father of Israel. She said, "That Old Testament God is not fair. Besides, my children are having trouble with this story. It's making them nervous about their relative safety in the sibling structure. They're not ready to hear it."

In fact they were ready to hear it, or they'd not have been experiencing anxiety.

Bible stories are not meant to make things easy for us. This is true of children as well as adults. The stories are meant to crack open the Word of God like a seed, a seed planted in our psyches and souls. The question is not "What does it mean?" but "How is this story unfolding today in the world around me? How is this story an event in my life?"

These questions and others like them inform the biblical storytelling of the Rev. Bill Dols of Myers Park Baptist Church, Charlotte, North Carolina, and form the foundation for the Bible Workbench of the Education Center, St. Louis.

How the decision is made as to what particular story you will tell, and when you will tell it, varies across denominations. Some churches are bound by a lectionary which assigns Scripture on a weekly basis. Other churches have more flexibility. Bill Dols speaks of the importance of telling a particular story at a particular moment for a reason. He speaks of making an effort to identify the teachable or preachable moment that reflects the life issues of the children.

Making it Happen

Don't hesitate to deepen a story with song, for example, or poetry...or interactive participation. Scripture is only as valuable to a congregation as its level of engagement.

The story of Hannah and Samuel and Eli, for example, is beautifully augmented by the Cursillo Hymn "Here I am, Lord." (*Songs: The Tune Book*, 209)

In a story like this, one narrator can do all three voices. Or assign the roles of Hannah, Eli, and God. Assign a mix of ages.

The children can stay with their parents for a story like this. It encourages the participation of the adults as well as the children, and discourages a dynamic often seen when children are in church, namely parents watching their children at worship.

For Relection:

- What is happening in the story?
- How is this story unfolding today in the world around me?
- How is this story an event in my life?
- These questions and others like them inform the biblical storytelling of The Rev. Bill Dols of Myers Park Baptist Church, Charlotte, North Carolina, and form the foundation for the Bible Workbench of the Education Center, St. Louis.

Begin by teaching everyone the chorus. Practice it once or twice.

Then strike the bell, don the Storyteller's Cloak, and begin.

HERE I AM, LORD

Narrator: A long long time ago in a town across the world, lived a woman named Hannah.
Poor Hannah. She was getting older and older...and she had everything she wanted, except for one thing. Hannah did not have a child. Not a single child. And you know what? The only thing she wanted in the whole world? A child.
What could Hannah do?
What do you think she did?

(The narrator might stop here to invite responses from the congregation.)

Well, first thing she did was cry a lot.
She'd go to the temple and cry.
Cried so hard, in fact, that Eli the temple priest thought she'd been drinking, but she hadn't.

Hannah: O Lord. I am so miserable.
I have no child.
I am old.
If you'd only give me a child, Lord, I would give him to serve you night and day in the temple.

Narrator: Well, guess what.
Hannah had a baby, and his name was Samuel.
And when Samuel was still in Hannah's belly, he sang this song.

Chorus: Here I am, Lord.
Is it I, Lord?
I have heard You calling in the night.
I will go, Lord,
If You lead me.
I will hold Your people in my heart.

Narrator: Samuel, as soon as he was old enough...twelve, I think... went to serve God in the temple, which was a good thing, because Eli the priest was getting very old. In fact, he could hardly see.

One night, Eli slept on his mat and Samuel slept on his mat. The voice of God came to Samuel.

God: Samuel, O Samuel. I am calling you, Samuel.

Be attentive to opportunities for intergenerational participation.

Narrator:	Well, Samuel was so surprised he ran straight to Eli, because he thought maybe Eli was calling to him. But Eli said:
Eli:	No, I didn't call you.
Narrator:	And before Samuel even realized what he was doing, he was singing the song that he'd sung when he was still in his Mama's belly. He sang it as he went back to his mat.

Chorus

Narrator:	Later in the night, the voice of God came to Samuel.
God:	Samuel. O Samuel. I am calling you, Samuel.
Narrator:	Samuel was half asleep, you know, and he ran right to Eli, because he thought Eli was calling him. But Eli said,
Eli:	Nope. I'm not calling you, Samuel. In fact, I've been trying to get some sleep. And I'd be doing it, too, if you wouldn't keep running in here.
Narrator:	Samuel went back to his mat, and the song just exploded from his chest.

Chorus

Narrator:	Guess what happened next?
	(The narrator might stop again, and ask for responses from the congregation.)
Narrator:	That same voice.
God:	Samuel. O Samuel. I am calling you, Samuel.
Narrator	But this time, instead of getting up and running to Eli, Samuel sat up, lit his candle, and began to pray.
Samuel:	Here I am, God. I'm listening.

Chorus

Narrator:	Did you know that when you sing God a song, it's like praying? God told Samuel that when he grew up he'd be a great prophet. What's a prophet, I wonder?

(The narrator might take advantage of another opportunity to teach.)

In fact, Samuel would be the greatest prophet in all of Israel. If...and this is really important...if, Samuel always told the truth about the visions he saw from God, good news or bad news, Samuel had to promise to tell the truth.

What do you think? Is this easy? Hard? Easy sometimes?

(The congregation may sing the entire song, or, depending on the time, only the refrain.)

Consider using another interactive technique. In its simplest form, an interactive reading consists of lector and congregation.

The value of Scripture read this way is that it invites close attention on the part of the congregation. The words to the right emphasize and deepen the content, sinking it down into the heart.

In this kind of interaction, children can stay with their parents.

The example below is an interactive reading in which the congregational response is indicated in the bold words to the right.

When working with children, exercise the freedom to stop the story for the sake of discussion. What's a prophet? (profit?) Never underestimate the value of that sort of conversation.

Isaiah 61: 1–3

The Spirit of the Lord is upon me,	**grace**
because the Lord has anointed me;	**chosen**
he has sent me to bring good news to the oppressed,	**gospel**
to bind up the brokenhearted,	**heal**
to proclaim liberty to the captives,	**release**
and release to the prisoners;	**freedom**
to proclaim the year of the Lord's favor,	**blessing**
and the day of vengeance of our God;	**power**
to comfort all who mourn;	**embrace**
to provide for those who mourn in Zion — to give them a garland instead of ashes,	**gift**
the oil of gladness instead of mourning,	**birth**

the mantle of praise instead of a faint spirit.	**strength**
They will be called oaks of righteousness,	**creation**
the planting of the Lord, to display his glory	**forever.**

The entire text of a reading done in this way will have to be included in the service leaflet.

As your congregation becomes familiar with this form of interaction, the lector may add hand and body movement to bring the reading into fuller dimension. For example, as she says, "the Spirit of the Lord is upon me," the lector brings her hands over her head and shoulders. As she says, "because the Lord has anointed me," she may lay her hand over her chest.

Develop gestures which reflect the meaning of the passage.

The instruction for a reading done this way can be accomplished in the moments just before church begins, because this is simple. This style lends itself well to the leadership of youth and children.

Consider a scriptural reading done with tableaux. A story in tableaux is a method of simple drama developed by Tom Long, director of Friends of the Groom, a group which adapts biblical stories for congregational dramatic presentation. Tableaux require minimal rehearsal (ten or fifteen minutes prior to the service) and work well with people of all ages.

A tableau, in this instance, is essentially a still life picture set with people. The operative word is still. Each time the congregation's eyes are open, there ought to be no movement in the tableau.

The example below is the story of the costly perfume. Use your bowl bell, or some other instrument, to sound the signal.

Again, children may stay with their parents.

The narrator gives instructions to the congregation. When you hear the sound of the bell, close your eyes. When you hear it again, open your eyes. Try it.

Close them. Open them. Close them. Open them.

Bowl Bell: Close your eyes

Narrator: Jesus came to a town called Bethany, where Lazarus lived. Maybe you remember, Jesus had raised Lazarus from the dead. There they gave a dinner for him. Martha served the food.

Bowl Bell: Open your eyes

(Tableau: Food on the altar, Martha pouring water from a jug, Lazarus, Jesus, and a couple others at the table.)

Bowl Bell: Close your eyes

Reader:	Mary took a large jar of expensive perfume mixed with oil.
Bowl Bell:	Open your eyes
	(Tableau: Mary is in front of the altar, smelling the oil. The rest are eating.)
Bowl Bell:	Close your eyes
Reader:	Mary anointed Jesus' feet with the oil and wiped them with her hair. The whole house smelled wonderfully with the fragrance of perfume.
Bowl Bell:	Open your eyes
	(Tableau: Jesus is in front of the altar, barefoot, with Mary next to him. She has anointed his feet, and is bending over his foot with her hair.)
Bowl Bell:	Close your eyes
Reader:	But Judas, who was about to betray Jesus, was angry. "You are wasting this perfume," he said. "Why not sell it for a lot of money and give the money to the poor."
Bowl Bell:	Open your eyes
	(Tableau: Judas has moved to the front of the altar and is shaking his fist in Mary's face.)
Bowl Bell:	Close your eyes
Reader:	Jesus said, "Leave her alone. She bought it so that she might anoint me at my death. You will always have the poor with you. You will not always have me."
Bowl Bell:	Open your eyes
	(Tableau: Judas is back at his place at the altar. Mary is holding both Jesus' hands and is weeping.)
Bowl Bell:	Close your eyes

Four to five tableaux in any given reading seem to work well, as far as the issues of simplicity and time constraints are concerned. With four or five pictures, the congregation as well as the participants seem to stay well focused.

Consider a scriptural reading done in parts. Again, this is an opportunity to work intergenerationally, and will hold the attention of the younger of the children, particularly if they comprise voices in the chorus, while the older children and youth and adults read the various roles. This is not a reading that requires a great deal of rehearsal time, and can be handed out just a few minutes before the service.

You may want to locate the voice of God in another place, the sacristy, for example, or another adjoining room.

First Narrator:	In the beginning, the earth was a formless void and darkness covered the face of the deep.
Second Narrator:	And a wind from God swept over the face of the waters.
God:	Let there be light.
Chorus:	And God saw that the light was good.
First Narrator:	God separated the light from the darkness. God called the light...
God:	Day.
Second Narrator:	And the darkness God called...
God:	Night.
Chorus:	And there was evening and there was morning, the first day. Gong (bowl bell).
God:	Let there be a dome in the midst of the waters, and let it separate the waters from the waters.
Chorus:	And it was so.
First Narrator:	God called the dome...
God:	Sky.
Chorus:	And there was evening and there was morning, the second day. Gong.
God:	Let the waters be gathered together into one place, and let the dry land appear.
Chorus:	And it was so.
Second Narrator:	God called the dry land...

God:	Earth.
First Narrator:	And the waters that were gathered together...
God:	Seas.
Chorus:	And God saw that it was good.
God:	Let the earth put forth plants and fruit trees.
Chorus:	And it was so. God saw that it was good. And there was evening, and there was morning, the third day. Gong.
God:	Let there be lights in the sky to separate the day from the night, lights for signs and for seasons and for days and years.
Chorus:	And it was so.
Second Narrator:	God called the light to light up the day...
God:	Sun.
Second Narrator:	And the light to light up the night...
God:	Moon.
Chorus:	God saw that it was good, and there was evening and there was morning, the fourth day. Gong.
God:	Let the waters bring forth living creatures; and let birds fly above the earth.
Chorus:	And God saw that it was good. God blessed them...
God:	Be fruitful and multiply and fill the waters in the seas, and let birds multiply above the earth.
Chorus:	And there was evening and there was morning, the fifth day. Gong.
God:	Let the earth bring forth living creatures of every kind, cattle and creeping things and wild animals of the earth of every kind.
Chorus:	And it was so, and God saw that it was good.
God:	Let us make humankind in our image, according to our likeness; and let them have dominion over the birds and the wild animals and over every creeping thing.

Chorus:	God blessed them....
God:	Be fruitful and multiply. Fill the earth.
Chorus:	It was so. God saw everything that had been made, and it was very good. And there was evening and there was morning, the sixth day.
First Narrator:	And on the seventh day God finished the work, and God rested. God blessed the seventh day, and hallowed it.
Chorus:	And God saw that it was very, very good. Gong.

When we can work intergenerationally with a story such as this, several things happen. We don't have the opportunity to misconstrue the drama as a performance. The congregation as a whole engages the story. If the adults feel a little silly at first, they soon lose that sense and become a vital and active part of the Word. And again, parents do not have the sense that they are watching their children at worship.

Have fun with Scripture, and by that I mean, engage Scripture with a sense of play. Sometimes changing the nature of the interaction with the biblical story allows us to hear it anew. Discover ways to let the Word convert you. Become a poet. You don't think you're a poet? Of course you are. Poetry was a form of spontaneous expression when you were a child, don't you remember?

> On top of old Smoky
> All covered with squash (corn, cheese, mud...)

Tell story in simple verse. Add a refrain to it and teach it to your children. Add a drum or a tambourine to keep the beat. Here's one I've told in many different contexts, the most recent being the most memorable. It was for a Service of Celebration of New Ministry, my own, at St. John's Church in Roanoke, Virginia.

I asked three fifteen-year-old boys if they would do this story in "rap" form. They agreed and we set out to rehearse. The rehearsal went badly. Finally they told me that my "rap" style must have come out of Ozzie and Harriet days (which it had) but that I needn't worry. They'd take it home and fix it by the next day. They did. The three boys arrived with sunglasses, baseball caps turned backwards, and a drum machine. They did this piece like it's never been done before. It was magnificent.

This is simple verse. It doesn't rhyme. It's syllabic content is inconsistent. It is easy to write, which you will discover as soon as you sit down outside under a tree with a lapful of felt pens, your dog with her head across your feet, and the birds of the air above your head singing their encouragement.

For Reflection:

- Do you think you're a poet?
- Of course you are. You have been a poet since you began to speak.

The refrain guarantees that your congregation will remember the disciple who doubted.

DOUBTING THOMAS
(Rap Sermon)

Peter was sitting in the upper room
with James and Andrew and John.
Thad-de-us was there
and Matthew, too
Along with Levi and Bartholomew.

And in comes Jesus
through the door which was closed.
Right into the middle of the room.
"No Way!" cried Peter, "You're supposed to be
lying in the cold stone tomb."

I DOUBT IT! is the word that everybody heard.
I DOUBT IT! I DOUBT IT!

"Don't be afraid," Jesus told his friends.
"Shalom be upon you today."
He blessed each one and when he came to the end,
He left the same way he came in.
Through the door...which was closed.

I DOUBT IT! is the word that everybody heard.
I DOUBT IT! I DOUBT IT!

Now in came Thomas, in from the street.
He'd been keeping an eye on things.
"We saw him! We saw him!" the disciples cried.
But Thomas shook his head as though they had lied.
And looked around for a little something to eat.

I DOUBT IT! is the word that everybody heard.
I DOUBT IT! I DOUBT IT!

"You're telling me that Jesus just walked in the room.
Through the door which wasn't even open?
You expect me to believe
that Jesus is alive
The same Jesus whose body was broken?"

I DOUBT IT! is the word that everybody heard.
I DOUBT IT! I DOUBT IT!

"I need to touch the holes in his hands and his feet.
The holes where they put those nails.
I need to put my hand right in his side

and then I can know for sure that he died
Because..."

I DOUBT IT! is the word that everybody heard.
I DOUBT IT! I DOUBT IT!

There was a hush in the air
and Jesus was there.
Thomas had tears in his eyes.
"Lord, is it you? How can it be?
Don't you know I was there when you died?"

I DOUBT IT! is the word that everybody heard.
I DOUBT IT! I DOUBT IT!

"Thomas, don't you fear. There's a mystery here.
And we all have a big part in it.
Death isn't the end, my doubting friend,
Death is only just the beginning."

I DOUBT IT! is the word that everybody heard.
I DOUBT IT! I DOUBT IT!

"Thomas, put your hands in the holes in my feet
And put your other hand in my side.
It's true what I tell you. I've risen from the dead."
Thomas was so happy that he cried.

Now tell me the word that everybody's heard.
I BELIEVE. I BELIEVE. I BELIEVE. I BELIEVE. I BELIEVE. I BELIEVE.

Scriptural Themes

Consider extracting themes from some of our powerful biblical stories and engaging a theme with a particular pastoral concern in your congregation. My suggestion is that you seek out and forge links between Scripture and pastoral care. They quicken each other, make both come alive.

Sometimes we tell the biblical story itself. Other times we work from its themes.

The Holy Family congregation works hard on issues of racism and homophobia, particularly with its children. It's a congregation that teaches inclusion, preaches inclusion, and reaches into the community in real ways, always building relationships.

Consider the question raised in the story of the Confession of Peter (Mt 16:13ff), "Who am I?"

The sermon which follows works from themes and draws on the "rap" style of the prior illustration. Again, it's a simple refrain that invites the focus and the participation of the congregation, both adult and child.

WHO AM I?
(Rap Sermon)

Who do you say that I am
that I am?
I am who I am who I am.

An elephant came to the church one day.
He said to the preacher, "I've come to pray."
But the preacher shook his head as if to say
"No way, Jose, be on your way."

"Whatever is the matter," the elephant cried.
"You think I can't fit in the chair?"
"It's not the chair," the preacher sighed,
"It's the air.
"Your ears are too big, they'll swallow all my words.
And the people won't hear a thing.
They won't hear the sermon and they won't hear the prayers.
And they won't hear the music to sing."

"They don't hear you anyway," the elephant said.
"They don't even pay attention.
But while we're on the subject of my ears anyway,
here's something that I thought I might mention."

Who do you say that I am
that I am?
I am who I am who I am.

Now Raggedy Ann went to the symphony.
She walked to the window for her ticket.
"I'd like a front row seat so I can feel all the heat
of the drums and the bass and the wickymajiggett.
I want to sit up close to see the sounds
I want to taste the violin.
I want to clap when the fiddler makes his rounds.
I want to watch them all pile in."

"You can't sit up front," said the ticket head.
"You're a distraction! Your hair's too red.
The drummer won't beat and the fiddle won't fiddle.
They'll have their eyes on you. You'll be in the middle."

"It just won't do," he shook his head sadly.
Raggedy Ann was feeling kind of badly.
But she opened her mouth..."While I have your attention,
There's something here I think I might mention..."

Who do you say that I am
that I am?
I am who I am who I am.

Don't be afraid to call on the adults. Remind them that it is not only their children who are discovering God. They too are in the process of discovering God.

For Reflection:
- Can you begin to see that the simple decision to include children in worship begins to take on a life of its own?
- Can you begin to see that the "next steps" are self-revealing?

My Daddy went knocking on the clubhouse door.
He said to the man, "You got room for one more?
I'd like to be a member of your organization.
If I were one of you, you could take a vacation.
I could answer the phone. I could dictate a letter.
I could greet the Queen or even do better.
I could raise a lot of money for the kids on the street.
Cook a lot of stew so the homeless could eat."

The man in charge shook his head back and forth.
"It's a good idea, but you're not of any worth.
You see your skin's too dark, and it just won't do.
The people inside won't think a lot of you."

My Daddy looked down and then he looked around.
He caught my eye with a wink.
"Here's the deal," he said to the man at the head.
"It really doesn't matter what you think."

Who do you say that I am
that I am?
I am who I am who I am.

Questions can serve to crack open the Good News carried in a sermon such as this.

What was the elephant trying to tell the preacher?

How did Raggedy Ann feel when the ticket taker said her hair was too red?

Why did the Daddy tell the man in charge, "It really doesn't matter what you think?"

The conversations that take place after the sermon itself can deepen the power of the experience.

Pose questions of your material. If you have a child who responds, "Even the rose left on the branch will die," there is no need to shrivel up or even let that be the last comment. Form that into a question.

"Uh oh. We have a flower cut off the vine, and we have one on the vine. Both of them die. Why then, I wonder, does Jesus tell us to stay connected to the vine?"

Don't be afraid to call on the adults. Remind them that it is not only their children who are discovering God. They too are in the process of discovering God.

Add a Child's Voice

Children love the stories of the Exodus. Take advantage of that. Construct a desert. Ask a member of your congregation who has both

For Reflection:

- During your worship over several consecutive weeks, consider who is not with you? Are there youth at worship? Children? Elders?

- If your congregation has a racial or ethnic predisposition, is that an accurate reflection of your local community?

tools and patience to build the thing. Make it an after-church project some Sunday, and be prepared to haul it into the church the next time you tell a desert story.

Build a simple box, say two feet square, with a bottom of thin pressed board or eighth-inch plywood. Add the Wilderness of Zin, the Negev, namely sand, or even kitty litter. Add a rock, the rock at Meribah. Fashion Mount Sinai out of papier mâché or foam rubber which has been painted. Populate it with people, animals, tents.

When we bring out the desert at the gospel, a child will invariably say, "Oh good! I love Moses stories."

Heather, seven, once asked, "Did Moses have any children?"

"Probably," I said. "Are you interested?" Yes, Heather was interested.

In fact, Moses did have a child, a son; he named him Gershom, because, in Moses' own words, "I have become an alien living in a foreign land." I told this to Heather.

"Well, did Gershom go down into Egypt with Moses to get the Israelites out?"

"I don't think so, Heather. I know his brother Aaron went along, and his sister Miriam shows up later, but I don't remember Gershom going along."

Whether or not Moses had a child, and whether or not that child accompanied Moses on his way to Egypt, wasn't really the heart of Heather's question. The question as I understood it was, "Where were the children?"

Well there had to have been some kids out there with Moses and the people of God.

Start to develop parts for children in the biblical narratives. Tell a story from a child's point of view. This is easy to do, and it allows a faithfulness to the text while at the same time it draws children and adults alike into a richer appreciation. Our first biblical child was a young girl named Yena who accompanied Moses on the flight from Egypt, sometimes walking alongside, sometimes riding on Moses' broad shoulders. Yena was there when the manna came down from heaven.

In this first of two examples of developing children's parts, I make use of a conversational technique which comes from Jerome Berryman, the founder of Godly Play, who uses the two simple words, "I wonder."

I wonder how they felt, the people of God who were slaves in Egypt. The children will tell you. They soon learn that the "I wonder" is their cue, their invitation to add their thoughts to the story as it develops. Once comfortable with the technique, you will find that the children will have plenty to share with the storyteller.

The idea is to draw out from the children what the experience might be like, giving the body and heart and soul a chance to respond before the intellect takes over.

YENA EATS THE MANNA. AT LAST.

A long time ago, thousands of years ago, the people of God followed Moses out of Egypt across the Red Sea and into the desert.

They followed Moses because God had sent Moses to get them. And they followed Moses because they didn't want to work so hard anymore. They'd been slaves in Egypt, and they'd built houses out of mud which they dug from the ground, and their backs hurt.

Have you ever seen people working like that...all bent over?

I wonder how they felt, those people of God.

I wonder how Yena felt.

Who was Yena? Yena was seven when Moses came to take the people of God out of Egypt. Seven. And she was very smart. When Moses said the word "freedom," Yena said, "How soon can we get out of here?"

Yena walked right up front with Moses. She was keeping her eye on things, making sure that he went the right way.

And when the waters of the Red Sea parted, Yena laughed and laughed and ran right on through.

Hadn't they fled their captors?

Hadn't they left the dry Egyptian desert behind? No more dust. No more sand.

Hadn't they crossed through the waters?

I wonder how Yena felt when her sandals touched the hot desert sand on the other side.

I can tell you what I think.

I think at first she was happy. Then she was angry.

I also think she was hungry.

She'd been promised a land of milk and honey. She'd been promised figs and grapes and lamb roasted with almonds.

What else, I wonder, had Yena been promised?

She'd been promised all that, and what she got was more desert. Hot dry sand and no food. None. Zip.

Yena turned to face Moses. She had to look way up to catch his eye. "You should have left us where we were," she shouted at him. "At least there was plenty to eat."

And pretty soon, all the people of God started to yell the same thing. "You should have left us alone. You should have left us where we were. At least there was plenty to eat."

And they could hardly sleep, with their bellies growling.

God heard their grumbling, of course, and God told Moses a secret. "There'll be food for them in the morning."

Morning came, and scattered across the desert was a blanket of white flakes. Some said like snow. Others said like coriander seed. Moses told them to eat, and they did.

All except Yena.

"Gross," said Yena, and she covered her head with her blanket.

"It's bread God sent from heaven," said Moses. "Eat it."

"It's not bread. It's not even close to bread."

The others all ate it. They said it was manna. They didn't rave and tell her it tasted like fresh roasted chicken with corn on the cob. But they told her she might as well eat some, seeing as how there wasn't anything else.

"Nope," said Yena. That girl was stubborn. She wasn't going to give in.

But Yena was smart, remember? And she had an idea. If those flakes that some said looked like snow and others said looked like coriander seed were coming out of the sky sent by God, then she'd just take her basket over the hill, out of sight of the camp, and just catch some of those flakes and take a bite or two when no one was looking. That's what Yena would do.

See, Yena was getting really hungry.

So...early the next morning, just before the people of God started to wake up, Yena sneaked away, to retrieve her basket.

I wonder how Yena felt, sneaking away to get her basket of manna?

But when she got there, it was empty. The manna had all melted away. Yesterday's was gone, and today's hadn't yet come. Now what was Yena to do?

She stumbled back to the camp. Stumbled because she was sad and stumbled because she was mad, and stumbled most of all because she was so hungry.

"Hey, Yena," cried her family and her friends. "Do you want to try some this morning? Do you want to taste the manna?"

Yena shook her head. "Yuck," she said. "Gross."

But Moses saw a tear in her eye and saw her lip quiver. He put his arm around her, so she wouldn't shiver. He wanted to help her, but there was nothing he could do. You see, the manna only came once a day, and it only fell where the people camped.

Poor stubborn Yena was getting very thin. In fact she seemed to be disappearing.

Early the next morning, very early the next morning, as the sun was only beginning to think about sending its rose pink rays over the top of Mount Sinai onto the desert, Moses tapped Yena on her foot, which had escaped from her blanket. Yena sat right up with her fist clenched, like she was going to belt him one.

He put one finger to his lips and said, "Sh-h-h. Come with me."

Yena and Moses slipped out of the camp before anyone was up. They walked out into the desert, still dark except for the faint glow of the sun climbing the back side of Mount Sinai.

"Where are we...?" Yena began. But again, Moses put his finger to his lips. "Sh-h-h."

So they sat there, the two of them, on the still cool sand. And as the sun peeked over the top of the mountain, the sky opened up and down came flakes and flakes and flakes of manna.

"Try it," said Moses. He was smiling.

And Yena did.

Yena ate the food of God that day, and she ate it every day after that. "It's not so bad," she would say when anyone asked. "Kind of grows on a person, if you give it a chance."

I wonder how the food tastes, the food that God gives us.

"I wonder how Yena felt, sneaking away to get her basket of manna?"
For a deeper discussion from Jerome Berryman, see: *Young Children and Worship*, published by Augsburg Press.

Connecting the Old and New Testaments

For better and for worse, I was accepted as a first year seminarian with no biblical foundation whatsoever. I couldn't have told you the difference between the Old and New Testaments, nor that what Christians call the Old Testament was in fact the Hebrew Bible. I didn't know gospels from epistles. I didn't learn "septuagint" until midway through my second year.

As consequence, I never make assumptions about the biblical literacy of anyone.

So, when the opportunity arises to weave the fabric of our Judeo-Christian tradition, I pounce on it. This is as true of my work with children as it is with the adults.

What follows is a sermon sample that does three things: it makes the Judeo-Christian connections; it writes in the voices of the children; and it allows the children their rightful prophetic voice.

UNTIL WE ARE SATISFIED

It was day one.

Moses and the people of God were wandering in the desert.
It was hot.
They were thirsty.
There was nothing to drink.
They were hungry.
There was nothing to eat.
The people grumbled against Moses.
They grumbled against God.

AT LEAST WHEN WE WERE SLAVES IN EGYPT WE HAD SOMETHING TO EAT.

From the midst of the crowd, the voice of a child floated on the air:

I DECLARE GOD WILL FEED US UNTIL WE ARE SATISFIED.

The people looked at the child. They thought s/he was crazy.
The next morning the ground was covered with a fine powder and the people ate their fill. They called it manna from heaven. Bread from heaven.

It was day two.

Moses and the people of God were wandering in the desert.
It was hot.
They were thirsty.
There was nothing to drink.
They were hungry.
There was nothing to eat.

For Reflection:

Consider our Christian inclination to separate the New Testament from the Old Testament. Where is our health and power if we divorce ourselves from our ancestral voices?

The people grumbled against Moses.
They grumbled against God.
AT LEAST WHEN WE WERE SLAVES IN EGYPT WE HAD SOME-THING TO EAT.

From the midst of the crowd, the voices of two children floated on the air:

I DECLARE, GOD WILL FEED US UNTIL WE ARE SATISFIED.

The people looked at the children. They thought they were crazy.
The next morning the ground was covered with a fine powder and the people ate their fill. They called it manna from heaven. Bread from heaven.

It was day three.

Moses and the people of God were wandering in the desert.
It was hot.
They were thirsty.
There was nothing to drink.
They were hungry.
There was nothing to eat.
The people grumbled against Moses.
They grumbled against God.
AT LEAST WHEN WE WERE SLAVES IN EGYPT WE HAD SOME-THING TO EAT.

From the midst of the crowd, the voices of four children floated on the air:

I DECLARE, GOD WILL FEED US UNTIL WE ARE SATISFIED.

The people looked at the children. They thought they were crazy.
The next morning the ground was covered with a fine powder and the people ate their fill. They called it manna from heaven. Bread from heaven.

It was day four, day five.

Moses and the people of God were wandering in the desert.
It was hot.
They were thirsty.
There was nothing to drink.
They were hungry.
There was nothing to eat.
The people grumbled against Moses.
They grumbled against God.
AT LEAST WHEN WE WERE SLAVES IN EGYPT WE HAD SOME-THING TO EAT.

As the story progresses from day four to day five thousand and five, the connection across the centuries is firmly established.

From the midst of the crowd, the voices of six children floated on the air:

I DECLARE, GOD WILL FEED US UNTIL WE ARE SATISFIED.

The people looked at the children. They thought they were crazy.

The next morning the ground was covered with a fine powder and the people ate their fill. They called it manna from heaven. Bread from heaven.

It was day five thousand and five.

Jesus led the people of God to a hillside.
It was hot on the hillside.
The people were thirsty.
There was nothing to drink.
They were hungry.
There was nothing to eat.
The people grumbled against the disciples.
The disciples grumbled against Jesus.
YOU BROUGHT US OUT HERE WHERE THERE IS NOTHING TO EAT.

From the midst of the crowd came the voice of a child, a child so tiny that you could hardly hear him.

I DECLARE, JESUS FEEDS US UNTIL WE ARE SATISFIED.

Another child added her voice to the first.

I DECLARE, JESUS FEEDS US UNTIL WE ARE SATISFIED.
More children and more children and more children...

I DECLARE, JESUS FEEDS US UNTIL WE ARE SATISFIED.

One of the children brought his basket of five loaves of bread to Jesus. Jesus thanked him. He blessed the bread, and he broke it. Guess how many people he fed with those five loaves of bread?

I wonder what you think about that. How could five loaves feed five thousand people?

I DECLARE, JESUS FEEDS US UNTIL WE ARE SATISFIED.

Trouble-Shooting

I once accompanied my friend Lisa and her children to a Quaker Meeting, the greater part of which was held in silence. Her children were ten, six, and four respectively, and they sat in comfortable quiet. I had never seen children sit in comfortable silence, didn't believe children could.

"God will feed us until we are satisfied," is a simple theological statement which opens a conversation about trust and surrender. The repetition of the phrase sends the message deep inside.

I know now they can be taught to sit silently. I know now that children will sit in silence in order to experience the mystery of God.

Again, a bowl bell becomes useful. The bell at Holy Family Church is a twelve inch diameter brass bowl with a striker. The sound that the bowl makes when struck is a single tone which resonates for perhaps twenty seconds. It is used not only for storytelling, but also for meditative occasions, including contemplative prayer.

I discovered, one day, that when I struck the bell, children and adults alike grew silent. Surprised by the consistency of response over time, I asked one of our children why he always became quiet.

"God's in the bowl," he said.

The matter-of-factness of his comment as well as the content of it, allowed me access to the thorniest of problems: noise management, an ever present factor when your worshiping community includes its children.

How do you draw children into moments of reverence and awe—never mind what adults call "appropriate church behavior"—without trampling the exuberance of their celebratory style? It's a question to be addressed in all aspects of worship, not only during the sermon.

"God's in the bowl."

That's a theology with some promise. If God's in the bowl, then when that bowl resounds, we'd better listen.

With that, the "Lark and Poppy" sermons were born, an example of which follows.

Poppy is six years old. She has long dark brown straight hair. She is a serious child. She loves to read. She loves to think. She loves the quiet. She loves her solitude.

Her sister Lark is four. Lark's hair is wildly curly. As her name suggests, she loves to sing. "I am made for singing," she says. Lark sings and dances her way through life.

Lark and Poppy more often than not find themselves bumping up against each other and are forced to negotiate those pieces of their lives they hold in common.

Children and adults both love the Poppy and Lark stories. Sometimes they identify with one or the other with great clarity. Other times they see themselves as a combination of the two.

Families make use of the Lark and Poppy stories at home, as a way to frame personality differences among siblings...between parents and children.

This first Lark and Poppy story focuses on the mystery of Shalom.

SHALOM

Lark and Poppy were sisters, any two more different children it would be hard to imagine.

Lark was four years old and her Mama must have known what to name her, because all this child wanted was to sing her way through her life.

She sang between bites of her breakfast bread. She sang between swallows of milk.

She sang on the way to the house of her teacher, and she sang as she fed hay to the cows.

Lark sang as her Mama washed her hair and her back and her feet, and she sang in her sleep.

Poppy was six, and she was missing several front teeth. Poppy loved the quiet. She loved to shut her eyes and listen to the sounds the wind made. She loved the earliest part of the mornings, before the people were up. She loved the sounds of the goats on the stones and the birds fussing and chirping in the olive trees.

Poppy loved her sister, as well, but she wasn't quite so excited about the racket Lark made.

"Besides," she would say. "She can't even carry a tune."

Most of all, Poppy loved the ocean, where Mama's brother Jack lived.

Two times a year they'd visit.

Poppy would run to the sandy shore. She'd throw her arms into the air. Shut her eyes and...just listen. Listen to the wind and the crash of the waves.

Not Lark. Lark would sing and shout and laugh and clap her hands and dance all over the sand.

Poor Poppy couldn't hear a thing. Except Lark.

"Lark!" Poppy had to shout to get her attention. "Lark! Can't you just be quiet and listen?"

"I don't think so," sang Lark. "It's too beautiful. The only thing I can do is sing."

"Yes it's beautiful," answered Poppy. "That's exactly the point. And the only thing I can do is listen. But how can I listen with you making so very much noise?"

It was a good question.

"God wants me to sing," cried Lark.

"God wants me to listen," argued Poppy.

Suddenly...from way in the distance...came a new sound.

Gong (Bowl bell).

"What was that?" Poppy wondered.
Even Lark was quiet.

Gong.

Then Poppy had a brilliant idea.

"I'll tell you what," she said. "Every time we hear that noise, you have to be quiet, so we can hear what's behind it. Agreed?"

Lark had to think about this for a minute. "What if I'm singing too loud and I can't hear it?"

Poppy was worried about this, too. But she thought maybe it was God's song, and if it were God's song, then she was pretty sure Lark would hear it.

"Don't worry," she said. "You'll hear it."

Gong.

Gong. Shalom. Peace be with you.

For Reflection:

What might be the experience of your community if your children were as ready to engage in theological conversation as they were, say, in conversation about video games?

Gong. Shalom. Peace be with you.

Poppy smiled. It was indeed God's song. Lark laughed out loud. It was God's song, and she thought maybe, just maybe, it was at least as pretty as her own.

Godly Conversations and Congregational Transformation

I was not the seminarian of my earlier story, the one who feared preaching to children because they always ruined the point. But I could have been. If I had to evaluate my earlier sermons with children, I would say that they were fast-paced, not the meandering conversations I've been describing, and deliberately entertaining. Most of all, they allowed me to be in charge. I took advantage of a captive audience, not so much out of a need to control, but more out of trepidation and intimidation. What if they asked something of me that I couldn't answer? What if I had to come up with something and I couldn't? What if I had to address something for which I was not prepared?

The process toward what I want to call "Godly conversation," as opposed to canned sermons, was several years in the making. It's not easy to let go. And there was no convincing me then, that in time I would be more comfortable in conversation with children than I ever was preaching to them.

Now I often prepare "focus" questions for a conversation I hope will happen. Often it is a conversation I believe will stretch our children, and I always tell them, "You're going to have to work very hard today."

As often as not, the children jump onto the questions and I throw my prepared work away. For the children of Holy Family, too, this was an evolutionary process. You can tell the children who have grown accustomed over the years, to having their thoughts and their theology acknowledged and honored. They are quick to speak, and they speak from a deeply thoughtful and insightful place.

They quickly make new children welcome and encourage their participation. They bring their friends.

Conversation with children engages the entire congregation. It is possible to share with one another, through Scripture and personal story, the work and presence and grace of God in our lives. Perhaps this sounds obvious to you, but it is not often my experience that adults and children together can participate in this way.

Families who can have those conversations together in church, are the families that take those conversations home.

Children who have these kinds of conversations in the church are the children who can have them outside.

What follows is an example of what I want to call a "Godly conversation."

Remember Harriet, in the woods, on her belly. "Sh-h-h," she tells us. "Listen. Wait. Wait in the dark."

Look for ways to build in adult participation. Worship can err on the side of its child-focus if the intergenerational opportunities are overlooked.

PSALM 139

I want to read something to you from the Bible. It's part of a psalm, and it goes like this.

Darkness is not dark to you, O Lord. The night is as bright
as the day. Darkness and light to you are both alike.

Darkness and light to you are both alike. How might that be? What about that?
Tell me about the darkness.
What do you find in dark places?
Scary things.
Night animals, owls, cats, seeds underground.
And what do seeds do in the dark?
Dreams. You find dreams in dark places.
Roots of trees. And what do roots of trees do in the dark?
What about in the dark of night? Stars, moon.
Candles in a dark room? A fire in the fireplace?
What about in the dark of your mama's belly? Do you think joy might have lived there?
What about hope? Can hope live in the dark?
Tell me how that might happen.
What about love. Can love live in the dark?
Can peace live in the dark?
I tell them about my daughter Heather's tree. Peace lives there.

Darkness is not dark to you, O Lord. The night is as bright
as the day. Darkness and light to you are both alike.

Dark is a word that we use to mean more than itself.
We might talk about a dark period in our lives. What might that mean? How can we bring in hope and love and peace and joy? Ask. Ask Jesus to be with you, because that's what Jesus brings into the world.
Jesus brings in himself, the light of God.
We talk about the Dark Ages. A time of war and chaos. Sickness.
But some people asked the light of Christ to come in, and it did.
People hid books, art, paintings, and music, so that we still have them.
Good Friday, the day Jesus died on the cross, is a dark day.
But what happened? The light of God came into that darkness and God raised Jesus from the dead to new life.

Darkness is not dark to you, O Lord. The night is as bright
as the day. Darkness and light to you are both alike.

At first blush, children may focus on the darkness as the context for scary things, but they won't stay there. You as storyteller have a powerful opportunity to hold up the darkness as the ground of new

All you have is the Spirit as she confers her authority on first one, then another, of the participants. This experience is not unlike preaching to a barren fig tree. The task is to listen.

life and the matrix of creation. The dark empty places of surrender are the foundation for the work which we do here. The dark empty places inside us are the seat of God's love.

Drama

Children in church form as varied and diverse a population as any. It is important, therefore, to be attentive to the kinds of participation that attract children who are different from one another, and the kinds of participation that attract children at different ages. By the time children reach the middle years (eight, nine, ten), they want to write their own plays. The children of Holy Family and I would sit together, sometimes on the beach, sometimes at Burger King. If it was a drama for a particular feast day we asked questions of the story.

For example, during Epiphany, the conversation around the Matthew story went like this.

"Herod wanted the wise men to do his dirty work."

"Yes, I'd say so."

"But they didn't want to do it."

"No."

"They didn't fall for his plan."

"No."

"What if Herod had gone himself to the stable? Would he have killed the baby?"

I can begin to feel the energy develop around this story. It is always an exciting moment. It's also a moment that you cannot plan, cannot foresee. It is a moment of grace, out of your charge, out of your control. A moment of grace that invariably comes.

"That's a good question. If Herod had tried to see the baby, how would the people know he had evil in his heart? How would they know to keep him out?"

We kicked these questions around for a while. Finally, one of the children said, "I know. They'd interview everyone who came to visit Jesus in the stable."

The children begin to shift from a story of long ago to one that is taking place right now. Our Epiphany play, drafted originally on Burger King napkins, is called *The Interviewer*. This kind of drama development can be a nerve-wracking experience. You don't have a story line. You don't have a plan. You don't know how it will turn out. You don't even know the characters.

All you have is the work of the Spirit as she confers her authority on first one, then another, of the children. The experience is not unlike preaching to a fig tree. Your task is to listen.

Then your task is to write. Get it down. Capture the passion of it. The editing can come later—and you will have to do some. But for the moment, try to capture the heart.

This play, like the one that follows it, is scripted as what we call an "accordion" drama. It can expand or diminish to accommodate more or fewer children.

The Interviewer is a play that has its "expansion factor" built in. The cast of characters whose single line, "A child is born!" can grow or diminish according to the number of actors.

THE INTERVIEWER

First Narrator: The Interviewer had once been nicknamed the BAD MAN OF KING HEROD THE GREAT. The Interviewer was King Herod's executioner, until one day he had a change of heart.

Interviewer: Too bad, old king. I can't do any more of your dirty work. I've had a change of heart, you see.

First Narrator: It made King Herod angry, and he drove the Interviewer out of Galilee and high into the hills, where his only company was his friend the Raven.

Second Narrator: The night was cold and dry. The Interviewer huddled deep in his cave in the high hills of Galilee. He wrapped his arms around his knees and knocked them together to keep warm.

First Narrator: There was a fuss in the town. Great excitement. An event. A secret.

Second Narrator: All the people in the town were talking. The secret floated on the air.

First Narrator: Even the Interviewer and his Raven, deep in the cave on the hillside could hear something. The Interviewer spoke to the Raven.

Interviewer: Go, my friend. Be my eyes and my ears. Tell me what has happened.

First Narrator: The Raven went as the Interviewer had bidden.

Second Narrator: Down in the town, the Innkeeper whispered to the milkmaid:

Innkeeper: A child is born.

Second Narrator: The milkmaid whispered to the oven cleaner:

Milkmaid: A child is born.

Second Narrator:	The oven cleaner whispered to the potter:
Oven cleaner:	A child is born.
Second Narrator:	The potter whispered to the goldsmith:
Potter:	A child is born.
Second Narrator:	The goldsmith whispered to the washer woman:
Goldsmith:	A child is born.
Second Narrator:	The washer woman, out late, rinsing the last of the laundry, whispered it to a star:
Washer woman:	A child is born.
Second Narrator:	And the Star...as we all know...was the Star of the East which had never been a star to contain herself, and so she shouted for all to hear:
Star:	A CHILD IS BORN! (Shout it out)
Second Narrator:	Kings heard it. Three Kings from the East heard it, and they started toward Bethlehem, bringing gifts. Shepherds heard it, and they wandered north from Judah and west from the Jordan. A court jester of Herod the King heard it and he made it into a joke, all this fuss about a child being born. Which is how King Herod himself heard it and decided to nip this child in the bud, which is another way to say he decided to kill it. King Herod wasn't too fond of children.
First Narrator:	The Raven who could go just about anywhere overheard King Herod planning to kill the child, and he flew back to the cave.
Raven:	A child is born. A special child. And Herod's coming to kill him. I heard it in the courtyard.
Interviewer:	But that's terrible news. Who is he sending?

First Narrator: The Raven shook his head back and forth, with much sorrow and fear.

Raven: That's just the point. No one knows.

First Narrator: The Interviewer thought and thought and thought. Herod had to be stopped. But how? How?

Interviewer: I KNOW. I'll interview them all. Everyone who comes to visit this child will have to come by me. I'll put them to the test.

Shepherd: I've come to see the child.

Second Narrator: Now this shepherd was a scruffy sort of guy. He had long hair and his hands were filthy. He had a hole in the toe of one boot, and to tell you the truth, he didn't smell so good. The Interviewer was suspicious.

Interviewer: O no you haven't. You haven't come to see any child. Not until you pass the test!

Shepherd: Test? What test?

Interviewer: If you had a hundred sheep and you lost one, what would you do?

Shepherd: Why, I'd go find it, of course.

Interviewer: You pass.

Innkeeper: I've come to see the child

Second Narrator: Now the Innkeeper had just cooked dinner for fifty-five travelers, and he was hot and red in the face. Plus he was dripping with sweat. Again the Interviewer was suspicious.

Interviewer: Oh no you don't. Not so quick there. You have to pass a test.

Innkeeper: Test? What test?

Interviewer: You were just sitting down to a meal, and it's the last food in the house. The last food in the town, even. And there comes a knock at the door. A tired family, hungry—starving, in fact—wants a bite to eat. What would you do?

"If you had a hundred sheep and you lost one, what would you do?"

A simple question like this can lead to dramatic presentations that provide the opportunity to incorporate more of our scriptural story.

For Reflection:

Many adults are bound by the "solemnity of worship." Can we give ourselves permission to laugh and enjoy our scriptural and liturgical heritage?

Innkeeper:	Why I'd give them my meal, of course.
Interviewer:	You pass.
King Herod:	(Dressed as rich lady) I've come...I've come to see the child.
First Narrator:	The woman was dressed in fine silks. She wore gold and diamonds. She smelled of perfume. The Interviewer, for once, had lost his tongue. He tried to point, but Raven blocked his arm.
Raven:	The test. The test.
Interviewer:	She doesn't have to take a test.
Raven:	The test!
Interviewer:	If a young woman with a baby in her arms stopped you in the street and begged you for a coin so that she could buy her child some milk, what would you do?
Herod:	(Falsetto.) Why I'd...Why I'd kick her in the shin to get her out of the way. And if that didn't work I'd hop in my carriage and have my driver run over her feet with the wheels.
Interviewer:	Out. Out. You fail the test. You're Herod. Out. Be gone!!!
Three Kings:	We've come to see the child.
Interviewer:	No, no, no. You can't fool me.
Three Kings:	But we've brought presents.
Interviewer:	What kind of presents?
Three Kings:	Gold. And Frankincense. And Myrrh.
Interviewer:	Okay then. You pass.
Herod:	(Dressed as a King) I'm with them.
Interviewer:	What gift have you brought?
Raven:	(Exposes a large sword.) Some gift.
Interviewer:	Out. Out. You're Herod. Get out. Be gone!

First Narrator:	There were many visitors that day, and the Interviewer tested them all.
Herod:	(Dressed as a baker.) I've come to see the child
Raven:	(Without speaking, simply turns the loaf around to expose a knife strapped to the back. Approaches Mary and Joseph and the baby.)
	Rise. Take the child and flee to Egypt. And remain there until I tell you.
	(The Holy Family gets up and exits down the aisle out the front door)

Use Your Plays Over and Over

Each year at Christmas we hear the words, "And it came to pass in those days, that there went out a decree from Caesar Augustus, that all the world should be taxed."

Whether it's the Revised Standard or the New Revised Standard Version, or the New English Bible, does not matter to me. I hear the words of the King James Version, as I have heard them all my life.

And with those words come the sights of too small kings with their too tall banners, the smells of brass and furniture polish, sounds of stage whispers and a shout or two of "Hurry up. We're going." Sights and sounds and smells of ritual as deeply embedded in my soul and psyche as any.

At Holy Family, we did some of our plays over and over. They became a part of the fabric of the shared life of the parish. The children knew to ask for them.

The children began to talk of our Easter drama somewhere around the forth Sunday of Lent. "Can I be MaryMag this year?" They remember.

Again, this is a play that can expand to meet the need and number of children. Disciples can be written in. Animals keep watch. Add a chorus.

The basic drama follows.

MARY MAGDALENE TEACHES PONTIUS PILATE A THING OR TWO ABOUT EGGS

MaryMag:	(Whistles and hums.)
Pilate:	Okay. So what have you done with him?
MaryMag:	Aren't you going to introduce yourself?
Pilate:	You know very well who I am. I'm Pontius Pilate.

MaryMag: Hmph. That's a funny name. I'm Mary. Mary Magdalene. You can call me MaryMag.

Pilate: So what have you done with him?

MaryMag: Who?

Pilate: Who? You know very well who. I'm talking about Jesus the King of the Jews. The one I handed over to be crucified. The One who died on the cross. That's who. What have you done with him?

MaryMag: Oh. He's not here.

Pilate: I can see he's not here. What have you done with him is what I'm asking.

(Mary Magdalene hands Pontius Pilate an egg from her basket.)

Pilate: What's this?

MaryMag: Looks a lot like an egg.

Pilate: Okay, okay. I can see that it's an egg. What are you doing with it?

MaryMag: I already told you. I'm Mary Magdalene. I always have eggs with me. Just in case.

Pilate: What does an egg have to do with the man who's supposed to be here but isn't?

MaryMag: (To the congregation) Such a mystery, don't you think?

Pilate: What does an egg have to do with Jesus who was killed and died on the cross and who was put in this tomb? I know because I saw it myself. What, may I ask, does an egg have to do with all of that?

MaryMag: You can always ask.

Pilate: I'm asking. I'm asking.

MaryMag: This egg is just like Jesus, after you put him in the tomb.

Pilate: This egg is like Jesus?

(Pilate scratches his head, and goes to sit on a rock. But the rock is having its own kind of fun, today, and it moves underneath him.)

For Reflection:

Resurrection theology can be problematic when taken from a cerebral perspective. As an exercise, how would you develop a Resurrection parable and share it with someone else?

Pilate: I don't get it. I still don't get it. What am I supposed to do now?

MaryMag: Are you hungry?

Pilate: What does that have to do with anything?

MaryMag: Well, I thought that if you were hungry, you might eat it, then you'll see what it has to do with Jesus.

Pilate: Hmm. Now that you mention it. I could do with a bite. Maybe I'll be able to think better after I've got a little something in my tummy.

(Pilate turns his back and through a sleight of hand, exchanges the white egg for a red plastic Easter egg that opens at the middle)

Pilate: A-A-AH!!! What happened? It turned red. How did it happen.

MaryMag: See? I told you. Just like Jesus. You took someone who was good and pure and clean in his heart and you killed him. Your egg is the color of his blood.

(Pilate goes again to sit on the rock, but the rock is still playing games and it moves.)

Pilate: Well, I'm still hungry. Can I eat it anyway?

MaryMag: Go ahead.

Pilate: But...but...but...No egg.

MaryMag: Well. Jesus is with God. Maybe your egg is, too.

Pilate: What am I supposed to eat?

MaryMag: Oh, we eat the food from a different table. This table here, in fact. (She points to the altar.) The bread and the wine. It's the food that Jesus left us.

(Pilate sits down on the rock: guess what?)

Teen Drama

The question is often put to congregations, "What are you doing for your teens? What programs do you have in place which are designed to keep your teens in church?"

However the question is posed, I think it's missing something.

A community is handicapped without the prophetic voice of its youth. Teens have an uncanny and unnerving ability to speak the reality of their lives, and those lives include the lives of their parents and the life of their community.

Our task as a congregation is to seek out and empower our youth to enrich and call into account the life we hold in common.

Teens are playwrights, too, and drama is a powerful vehicle for engaging youth in their daily struggles, particularly if drama and music (music of their choosing) can combine, in church, to crack open the Word of God in new ways, suspending church tradition of language, hymnody and physical constraint.

That may seem like a lot to ask of a congregation, but that's only if you don't yet understand your worshiping community as one which not only includes its teenagers, but as one which is willing to be challenged and revitalized by the power of its youth.

Keeping a group of teens focused is hard work, but not impossible. And you will always find one or two willing to help you with the tying up of things left unfinished. With teenagers, structuring a drama around popular music is often successful. At Holy Family, we created a play with a strong anti-drug message using music and some lyrics from "Counting Blue Cars" by the band, Dishwalla.

Rehearsals, too, are problematic. But I have discovered that what looks like a drama in chaos and shambles on the day before performance, becomes something altogether Spirit-filled on the actual day.

Expanding our Concept of Church

Church is everywhere.

Take the children of your congregation into your church, and ask them, "What is church?"

"Church is where you come on Sundays. It's where you see your friends."

Is Sunday the only time you come here? Oh, you go to school here, too. Is it the only place you see your friends?

So, what is church?

"Church is where you sing and pray."

Do you sing any place other than church? Like at home, or in school, or just outside?

What about praying, do you pray at home? At night?

So, what is church?

"Church is where you get bathtized. With water."

Given the chance, children really can tell you about church. They can tell you about quiet and prayer. They will talk about community, about family, about music and art and stained glass. They will talk about Baptism and Holy Communion.

Once the children of your congregation are this articulate about church, I would suggest that it's time to take them for a Sunday walk. Think of a special place, maybe a wooded trail, a pond, a flat place with tall grasses. You can do this during a Sunday service, or after, as a field trip.

Set it up in advance as a picnic and tell the children they can bring friends if they wish.

With the children of Holy Family, we did what we call a meditative walk. The children line up behind a leader who sets down one foot about every ten seconds.

The leader offers a meditation like this one.

The voice of the prophet is the voice that insists on the possibilities of transformation. The prophetic voice is carried powerfully in our youth, and when that voice is segregated or otherwise

For Reflection:

Once the decision is made to include the entire community in worship, the liturgy must begin to evolve. This is a good thing. Rather than attract a certain type of piety to itself, community worship must evolve to meet the ever deepening spiritual needs of the community.

Can you begin to think of liturgy in terms of a process of evolution?

As you walk, pay attention to the colors of the grass and the flowers, the leaves, the roots and the trunks of the trees. What do you hear? Birds? Insects? A plane overhead? Think about the soil under your feet. Is it spongy? Hard packed? What are you looking at? Pay attention to the wind as it bends back the blades of the grasses. Feel the sun and the wind on your cheeks, your forehead. Feel it ripple your hair.

Settle for lunch near a body of water, if you can, or have a water jug with you. Sing songs. Wash your hands. You might speak about being washed by the water of God as we are washed in Baptism. Give thanks for your meal, break bread, remember for a moment Jesus' walk on this earth, and remember his promise of the Holy Spirit. Share your meal. Then ask the children, so, what is church?

Church is where God is.

Is God here in this place? Yes.

Is this church? Yes.

We forget that church is about people. Church is about the whole community gathered for worship and praise, the mutuality of love and the exchange of service. If our focus is on the building and the linens and the order, then we tend to support the exclusion of children. We tend to relegate them to the basements where, in grown-up eyes, they can do no damage.

Commercial Literature

As we expand our concept of church, we need not focus on the space alone. Look to the myriad opportunities offered by commercial literature. Scripture is not the only way to break open our understanding of God and church and everything that is holy. What follows is a brief list of books that offer what I consider significant literary opportunity. There are other Holy Family favorites included in the Suggested Readings in Appendix B.

CREATION STORIES

In the Beginning There was Joy, by Matthew Fox, takes advantage of simple rhymes and fabulous colors to expand the biblical creation stories to include atoms and electrons and protons, galaxies, stars, and super novas. This book is a celebration of all life and roots itself in a generous and consistent ecology.

And God Created Squash, by Martha Hickman, is a work that explores the tactile, giving children a world of sight and touch and smell created by a whimsical God.

EARTH STORIES

A Prayer for the Earth: The Story of Naamah, by Sandy Sasso, tells the Noah story from before the flood until after the flood had receded, from the perspective of Noah's wife, whom God has named "Mother of Seed." Naamah's vocation is to carry seeds, two of every kind, onto the ark,

For Reflection:

Take a meditative walk with a group of children and adults. Savor the sensory experience in its totality. What is it like for you?

a task which she carries out faithfully. In the days following the flood, she re-seeds the earth, and God renames her Emzerah, Mother of Seed.

The Elders are Watching, by Dave Bouchard, with exquisite serigraphs by the artist Roy Henry Vickers, is a powerful witness to the woundedness of the earth and the instruments of the wounding. It is also a story of hope and redemption.

OTHER STORIES

Old Turtle, by Douglas Wood, is an award winner, with extraordinary art and a simple, clear, powerful message. It's a Tower of Babel story with a twist.

The whole creation of God knew God and knew they knew God. Each understood God from within her particular framework, and anything that fell outside a particular perspective could not be God.

The whole creation of God began to argue with one another, until Old Turtle, silent witness to the wounding of the world, called a stop to the chaos. She acknowledged each creature's perspective. Yes, she said, God is that, and more. Yes. And yes. And then Old Turtle warned about the people to come, people who would wound the earth still further before they could come to see God in one another.

In God's Name, by Sandy Sasso, does a similar thing, and acknowledges the many many names of God: Source of Life; Creator of Light; Redeemer; Healer. Again, the names of God fall within the perspective of the one doing the naming. Until finally, all the creatures of God understand God as One. This is critical. Have you ever noticed how quickly children pick up the male gender language about God, and how difficult it is, even at the formative moments, to expand that understanding? With those patterns set so early, is it any wonder that we have such a difficult time with the gender issues as we mature?

Lion and Blue, by Robert Vavra and Fleur Cowles, has become a Lenten tradition at Holy Family Church. It appears to be a book for children. The artwork and the artist are legendary. But it's not necessarily a book for children. It's a book about a journey, and therefore it's your story and it's my story. It's a story that belongs to all of us.

Lion in his jungle home is content enough, so the story begins, until one day an other-worldly, beautiful, blue Brazilian butterfly floats across his life. Lion loses his heart to her. She is the subject, object, and total content of his heart's desire.

Blue celebrates her time with Lion, but in the same breath she warns him, "Lion. One day I must leave you, to seek my Golden Sun."

Lion hears her, but their days are filled with the quiet joy of companionship, Lion lulled into an atmosphere of peace which nothing can rupture.

But one day he wakes, and Blue is gone, gone on her search for her Golden Sun. Lion can do nothing but follow.

Across the jungle and across the water, through fields of flowers, deserts of glistening sand, ages pass, and still Lion follows, seeking,

For Reflection:

Bring to mind a time at worship outside the context of a church building. What was it about that experience that made it church? What was it about that experience that was other than church?

yearning, aching for his Blue. Lion's journey is one of transformation, one of becoming. He is becoming himself the Golden Sun, carrying within his own heart all that is good and holy and sacred.

The fruit of his transformation, of course, is the reunion of Lion and Blue.

Widening Our Embrace

In 1996, Holy Family Church articulated a yearning to build a relationship with the Coastside Jewish Community.

The Coastside Jews had recently formed their organization and in the early stages, held a monthly Shabbat service out of various members' homes. As they grew in number, they outgrew their various living rooms and Holy Family offered them the use of the sanctuary.

On the nights of Shabbat, we removed or veiled what we loosely called "impediments to worship," namely the stations of the cross, the processional cross and the tabernacle. Our altar guild director sewed a six-foot-by-four-foot blue satin banner with a Star of David to veil the crucifix.

The friendship proved to be a rich one, and Holy Family Church soon discovered that a commitment to preaching with children actually became one avenue of deepening that relationship.

Again, it's a question of making the connections between our Judaic and Christian heritage. As children and congregations learn to honor the significant stories and experiences of the people of God, whether they lived before the time of Jesus or after, misunderstandings and misconceptions fall away.

These two sermons serve as examples which honor the history and faith stories of both communities. In the first example, the Transfiguration story is itself transfigured to lift up the persons of Moses and Elijah.

The storyteller begins with a very simple chant that s/he can teach a congregation in moments.

This one begins on G, and moves to A, then C, B and back to C.

THE TRANSFIGURATION

Storyteller:

Jesus went up the Mountain.   (CHANT)
Jesus went up the Mountain.
Jesus went up the Mountain.
And his face / shone / with the glo / ry of God.

There are other ways to sing this song and I'll give you examples.

Moses went up the Mountain.   (CHANT)
Moses went up the Mountain.
Moses went up the Mountain.
And his face / shone / with the glo / ry of / God.

Elijah went up the Mountain.   (CHANT)
Elijah went up the Mountain.
Elijah went up the Mountain.
And his face / shone / with the glo / ry of / God.

Storyteller:

That's a lot of people up there on that Mountain.
Why'd they all go up there, I wonder.
Well, let's start with Moses.

Why did Moses go up the Mountain?
God told him to.
To get the stone tablets...the Law... the Ten Commandments...

He talked to God and his face turned brilliant red, like being in the sun only hundreds of times hotter.
Why, do you suppose?
Anything else you want to say about Moses?

Moses went up the Mountain.   (CHANT)
Moses went up the Mountain.
Moses went up the Mountain.
And his face / shone / with the glo / ry of / God.

Storyteller:

Okay, Elijah the Prophet...
We know what a prophet is, right?
Sometimes the people don't really want to hear what a prophet has to tell them.
That was true of Elijah.
He told the King's wife whose name was Jezebel that she should stop worshiping idols and instead worship God.
Jezebel sent her soldiers to get Elijah, so he ran...and ran...
Ran right up that mountain to hide.
And a great wind came to the mountain, but Elijah couldn't find God in the wind.
And the great noise of the storm came to the mountain, but Elijah couldn't find God in the storm.
And then Elijah was quiet, so quiet.
He heard the voice of God in the quiet
and the voice said, "Elijah, do not be afraid."
How would you feel if you heard the voice of God telling you "do not be afraid?"

Storyteller:

Anything else about Elijah?

Elijah went up the Mountain.   (CHANT)
Elijah went up the Mountain.
Elijah went up the Mountain.
And his face / shone / with the glo / ry of / God.

When we first began to build our program of family worship, I understood—I should say misunderstood—my role as a storyteller. I believed that if I could entertain the children, they would want to come back. And of course they did. For about six weeks. Their spiritual hunger was such that they quickly outgrew stories designed to entertain. I began to look at stories and drama in the way that I should have all along, as the foundation blocks of our shared spiritual journey.

Storyteller:

Okay, now who's going up the mountain?

Jesus went up the Mountain.　　　　　　(CHANT)
Jesus went up the Mountain.
Jesus went up the Mountain.
And his face / shone / with the glo / ry of God.

Storyteller:

Jesus went up the mountain to pray.
And he took his disciples Peter and James and John with him.
And Jesus' face turned brighter than light, and his robes...
everything...dazzling white.
And God's voice from the heavens, "You are my child, my be-
loved."
And the strange thing?
Here come Moses and Elijah to be with him.
How can that be? They're already dead!

James and Peter and John wanted to build three booths,
so Jesus and Moses and Elijah could stay up there forever.

Jesus said no.
"My work is down in the valley, with all the people."
Anything else about Jesus?

Jesus went up the Mountain.　　　　　　(CHANT)
Jesus went up the Mountain.
Jesus went up the Mountain.
And his face / shone / with the glo / ry of God.

Because of our relationship with the Coastside Jewish Community, we acknowledge their High Holy Days and recognize other special feast days, in particular Yom Ho'Shoah, the Day of Holocaust Remembrance. Although this is not to say that you must preach a Yom
Ho'Shoah sermon, we chose to do that because of our relationship.

Jesus calls us into remembrance. "When you eat this bread and
drink this cup, do this in remembrance of me." Do this in remembrance
of the horror of violence and murder and evil that we do to one another.

Yom Ho'Shoah is a difficult remembrance, and it is important to
provide the kind of pastoral and emotional support that allows people
to speak, to comfort one another and to pray.

Look for opportunities to
build the bridges be-
tween the scriptural sto-
ries of the Old and New
Testaments.

For this sermon, we darkened the church and lit candles. We asked the children to sit with their parents. We spent time together afterwards, still in candlelight, talking softly among ourselves, singing songs from Taize.

If you do this, and it is a judgment call, it is important to set in place the supportive matrix out of which can come conversation, tears, and further work.

YOM HO'SHOAH

There was a war. The whole world was in it. You were either on one side or the other. There was no in-between. But the people who suffered the most were the Jews.

Tell me about the Jews.

The people of Israel.

Abraham and Sarah, Isaac, Rebekah, Jacob, Leah, Rachel.

Moses led the people of Israel out of slavery in Egypt to the Promised Land.

Jesus was a Jew.

In this war, the people who suffered most were the Jews.

What happens in a war, I wonder?

What happens to people?

What happens to families?

To the earth?

(This is opportunity for discussion with the whole community, not only the children.)

This war was called World War II. It was a very hard war.

Children were put in prisons

No food. No water.

No medicine.

Children died.

Light Prayer Candle Number One

Let's say a prayer for all the children of the world.

Dear God, we remember our children. Keep our children safe. Let them eat the food of the earth, and drink from the rivers and streams. Let them sleep at night without fear. Let them know love. Let them know joy. Let them know peace. Amen

In the prisons were the mothers of the children.

No food. No water.

They were beaten.

Most of them died.

Light Prayer candle Number Two

Let's say a prayer for all the mothers.

The point is to make the connections between the stories you tell and the relationships your community is building.

Dear God, we remember our mothers. We remember their courage. We remember their love. Fill their hearts with your tenderness. Fill their hearts with your peace. Amen

In the prisons were orphans.
What's an orphan, I wonder?
They were alone.
They were scared.

Light Prayer Candle Number Three
Let's say a prayer for the orphans.

Dear God. We remember all orphans. Orphans from the war. Orphans today. We remember all people who have no parents. Fill their hearts with your Spirit so they will not be alone. Embrace them within your love. Shower them with your peace. Amen

In the prisons were the elders.
What's an elder, I wonder?
Wise people.
Teachers. Rabbis.
They used to tell people how to live.
Now they had to teach people how to die.

Light Prayer Candle Number Four
Let's say a prayer for the elders.

Dear God, we thank you for the lives of those older than we are. Those with wisdom and understanding and compassion. We remember our elders. Fill them with your mercy and your steadfast love. Show them the power of forgiveness. Amen

Throughout the whole world, there were heroes.
What's a hero, I wonder?
People who helped one another.
People who hid the Jews.
People who kept them safe.
People who fought.
People who died.

Light Prayer Candle Number Five
Let's say a prayer for the heroes.

Dear God, we remember the heroes and we give you thanks. Fill us with their strength and their courage so that we may serve one another. Fill their hearts with your peace. Amen

Millions of people died.
Of those millions, six million Jews died.
Men, women, children.
Old people.

Sick people.
Millions of people. Six million Jews. Many others.

Light Prayer Candle Number Six

Let's say a prayer for the millions of victims who died in this war, and for all victims of violence and war.

Dear God, we remember today the millions of your people who were killed in World War II, Jews and non-Jews. We remember all who have been killed and all victims of violence. Let us never forget a people so ravaged. Teach us peace, O God. Amen.

In Closing

The fruit of preaching with children can be the transformation of an entire congregation.

We become different with each other. Adults learn to listen to the children. Children know and interact with all the adults, not only their parents. The free and easy banter between the youngest and the oldest of the Holy Family congregation is powerful witness to inclusive community.

Worship is taken in deeply, like air into the lungs.

The worship changed the Holy Family community.

The worship changed me.

The second Sunday of Advent, during the coffee hour between services, someone came up to me very discreetly, very gently. "Caroline." She tugged at the sleeve of my robe. "There's someone out here I think you might want to deal with before you get started with the next service." I glanced out the door where she was directing me. A man stood there, in the rain, sandals on his filthy feet, long hair, unkempt, things hanging from his coat as though he'd collected them from the street and then forgotten about them, like children collect things in their pockets.

I took a look and then I laughed. I'd invited him for our drama. "Oh, that's just John the Baptist."

I knew John the Baptist. Hadn't I been reading about him for years? And not only that, but here he was here at my own invitation, looking exactly as I'd told him to look. "Oh that's just John the Baptist, guest of honor at the family service."

The man who'd agreed to come to Holy Family Church to play this role was a friend from a neighboring congregation. No one knew him but me.

I knew John the Baptist. Knew him so well that I could tell him how to proclaim his mission, knew him so well I could tell him how to stage his entrance, knew him so well I could script his every word. We all know John the Baptist, or think we do, and somehow that gives us the privilege or right to tell him what he's to say and how he's to say it.

But the John the Baptist that spent time with Holy Family Church that Sunday of Advent, wasn't the Baptist I knew or had

My advice is simple. Just start. The deepening spiritual lives of the children of your congregation will impact the entire congregation no matter how this is accomplished. It can't help it. And it will change you forever.

scripted. Not a wild man, but a gentle one. Not a man confident in his special godly assignment, but a man who was awkward, shy, uncomfortable. He stuttered. At times he became incoherent.

We knew, or at least some of us did, and I suspect that because I already knew the script, I was the last to know, what John was saying to us. He told us that he was far more at home out in the desert, isolated from all but his own demons with whom he had grown quite comfortable, but he'd come in, reluctantly, as we all were witness, at the request of God, to do something on behalf of God's Kingdom, something that had to be accomplished. And out of some totally irrational process on God's part, the task had fallen to John himself.

John's charge was twofold: to clear a path and to make straight the ways of God, and to baptize his cousin Jesus. He didn't want to do either. Of course he didn't want to do it. He was unfit. Unprepared. Uncomfortable. Unwilling.

As he came in the room, he cleared the path, like he was instructed, but it was an altogether different kind of path than the one I'd scripted, different because none of the congregation behaved. John couldn't manage to clear the people out of the way. They and he together cleared a path of another sort altogether.

Rather than scatter, they put themselves directly in the path, greeted John as he made his way along the aisle to the front, and made him welcome, this bizarre looking hermit out of some desertscape, reluctant to come into the world.

And then, one child said to him, "Don't worry. It's not what's on the outside that counts. It's what's inside." The path that John himself had come to clear was prepared even more fully by this child, and between the two of them, they laid low enough mountains, straightened out enough crooked paths, that Jesus himself could make his way into our midst. Jesus himself, not the Jesus I'd scripted but a cool—as someone remarked later—Happy-Days-Fonz-cool Jesus, whose crooked kind of gentleness allowed John the room he needed to accomplish his part of the task.

For me, the experience was one of letting John and Jesus script themselves, and the result was an experience of exquisitely painful and almost intolerable joy.

The Holy Spirit confers her authority on any one, at any age, at any time, which is precisely why a worshiping community needs all its members.

But if your interaction with the children of your community takes place in some part of the premises other than the church, don't despair. Everything in this chapter, in this book, can correspond to your work with children in a more traditional Sunday school setting. Use that setting to your advantage. Invite people in. Let them listen. Let them hear the Word. Let them be changed.

My advice is simple. Just start. The deepening spiritual lives of the children of your congregation will impact the entire congregation no matter how this is accomplished. It can't help it. And it will change you forever.

Dear Mr. God

What, Me Pray?

Prayer is central to your church's community life and to your worship.

Over the eight years I served Holy Family Church, the children of the congregation taught me—or perhaps I should say reminded me—that adults, too, can build a prayer life with God and the community that breaks the constraints of customary prayer forms. Children pray with an intensity and a candor that serves to release all of us into a more dynamic and immediate prayer life. This has been true of the Holy Family congregation, and it will be true of yours as well.

I would categorize myself among the many of us who are "prayer bound." During my first year in seminary, I was invited to the sixtieth birthday celebration of a close friend. The invitation included dinner, and I was warned in advance that I would be asked to say grace.

I barely slept for the three days prior to the party. I was too nervous about the grace. At the time, I was comfortable enough with the Episcopal Book of Common Prayer, but ask me to offer prayer extemporaneously, and I disintegrated.

I wrote a prayer. Something about the privilege of friendship, the benefits of a sixty-year-old wisdom, and thanks for the food. I wrote it on a three by five index card, and then I memorized it. I put pauses in appropriate places, as though I were searching for words in the sacredness of the moment.

"You're a natural," my friend said later, thanking me for the prayer. "You couldn't have done better if you'd rehearsed it."

The children and youth of your congregations will ease, lead, and entice you into a life of corporate prayer that is personal, vital, deep, and compassionate. I suggest that they are natural ministers of prayer.

For Reflection:

- Take a moment with pen and paper to write down your prayer habits: when you pray; where you pray, etc.
- Share with a small group any awkwardness you might feel about extemporaneous prayer.

Holy Prayers

I am not sure when it began, but I learned to distinguish types of prayers from one another. There were prayers God would like. Dear God, please bring peace. That was a good one, so powerful in fact that I sometimes dared slip in a request or two for myself. Dear God, please bring peace, and how about picking me for starting pitcher on the team?

Prayers God wouldn't like. Selfish prayers. Prayers of condition. Dear God, if you let me win the class prize this year instead of Harriet....

Silly prayers. Dear God, don't make me laugh when Mrs. B. throws the chalk across the room. Or dear God, don't let the Tooth Fairy give Nancy a dime! Please God, let there be one more cookie left in the package.

Not only did I learn to distinguish types of prayer, I learned to rank them as well. The ones that were prayed to the benefit of another were of a higher order than the ones offered up for self. The ones prayed to the benefit of the world were on another level altogether.

Then there were what I called the saintly prayers. Dear God, help me to be kind and not talk back to Mom. Dear God, help me with my temper. Dear God, give me strength to wash the dishes without complaining.

By the end of orientation week, my first year of seminary, I had discovered an entirely new class of prayer. Holy prayers. These are the prayers with the right formulas. O Holy God, Transcendent and Imminent...Almighty and Everlasting Father, you rule the planets in their courses, fill our hearts with your grace, we beseech you.... Help us to cherish what you will....

I met people who popped off these prayers like you do your mother's maiden name on a bank form.

I was intimidated. Struck dumb might be a more appropriate description, in the face of such holy prayers from people unlike myself, who were clearly religious.

By the end of my first week of classes I had stopped praying altogether.

The Right Way

Much of what we do in liturgical churches supports the myth that there is a right way to pray. Adults are comfortable with prayer books, collects assigned for the day, with standardized prayers, say, for safety and travel, for the whole human family, for the earth, for those who are sick, and for those who mourn.

We are comfortable with the same prayers, week after week, year in year out.

Conversely, we are not comfortable with variations in prayer.

We are uncomfortable, some of us to the point of catatonia, with extemporaneous prayer. Many times I have asked for a prayer

It is a teaching moment when two children, playing soccer on opposing teams, each prays that God grant his team the win.

For Reflection:

- Talk with one another in a small group about the vitality of corporate prayer in your congregation.
- To what extent has your prayer life become automatic?

volunteer to begin a meeting, or an event. People turn away their heads, engage in rapid conversation, or stoop to tie their shoelaces.

Even when we scatter all caution to the winds and break free of our bondage to a given compilation of words, we cannot seem to shatter the chains of the forms of prayer and the order they prescribe, at least in some denominations. Pray for the church. Pray for the nation. Pray for the world. Pray for the local community. Pray for the sick. Pray for the dead.

Freedom

The prayers of children free us from insisting that there's a right way to pray.

The prayers of children free us from insisting that there's a right way to pray. In Chapter Six, "The Community of the Bathtized," Thomas, who was two and a half at the time, offers a baptismal prayer for his sister Grace and makes connection between food and Baptism and family:

> We thank you God
> for giving us this bread.
> We thank you for
> blessing our family.

Children talk to God about all kinds of things, and the ones that aren't yet talking draw pictures. Prayer is central. Every one prays. Holy Family Church offers "Prayer Packets" to families, each packet a stack of index cards tied with a ribbon the color of the liturgical season.

Families are asked to take them home and spend prayer time together, developing their intercessions and thanksgivings for the coming Sunday. This is a simple way to begin building the kind of partnership between church and family that can enrich the entire community. Some families are altogether rebellious and refuse to participate; others simply forget...all the time. Sometimes families forget some of the time. But some forget once or twice then begin to remember.

It's a great and simple idea that works imperfectly.

Sunday Morning Options

Given that not all families will bring prayer packets with them to church, and given the likelihood that there will be visitors, it's a good idea to make prayer cards available in the church on Sunday mornings. Designate a special prayer basket and fill it with pens, pencils, crayons, markers, and index cards.

Within the worship services of many congregations, there is a designated moment for the prayers, sometimes known as the Prayers of the People. When the children of your congregation become familiar and comfortable with prayer activity, they will offer prayers as the service of worship unfolds. Although many of the children will remember that there is a designated prayer time and offer their prayers then, or place them in the prayer basket as it comes by, young children in particular, anxious to deliver the concerns of their hearts to the priest or pastor, may bring prayer cards forward at almost any time.

Don't discourage them.

All prayers are critical prayers. As often as not, they will reflect the kind of day it's becoming; reflect what the children have heard in the Liturgy of the Word, perhaps the music. Reflect, perhaps, what they've overheard in casual conversation as people enter the church.

These prayers are spontaneous, immediate, and powerful.

The prayer life of the children will spill over into the prayer life of the entire community. Many of the children and adults of Holy Family compose several prayers on a given Sunday, either with words or pictures.

Some of them require creative interpretation on the part of the prayer leader, but I have not yet encountered a single child who is not pleased and willing to share her prayer intention.

At whatever moment your particular community designates as prayer time, children assigned to the task bring the prayer basket to the prayer leader. If you are that designated person, you know, as you receive the basket, that you've just been entrusted with precious gifts, namely the deep concerns of hearts offered to God.

One Sunday the first several prayers offered widened the embrace of the congregation to include family pets, the children of Haiti, the rain, certain endangered species, and Uncle Ed who died.

Prayer cards work especially well with younger children, and provide a way for them to contribute to the liturgical work of a congregation in tangible and significant ways.

Prayer cards work equally well with teens and adults. There is something about a blank card, a magic marker, and an overfull heart that dance well together.

During the opening night liturgy of the national conference, Charting a Course for Children and the Church, each participant was asked to offer, on a prayer card, her most precious prayer for the children she loved.

Those prayers were offered at the altar that evening, prayed the next morning, and then hung on the walls of the sanctuary for each of us to read.

Prayer is Ministry

Prayer is ministry, ministry of all kinds, and it is the ministry shared by all of us. Congregations must explore new ways to foster the ministries of their children.

Included here are a broad selection of prayers which the children of Holy Family Church have agreed to share.

Ministry of Pastoral Care

Prayer offered up in the moment serves as a window through which an attentive pastor can gauge the health of his or her congregation. Prayer serves as an indicator of a change in the family dynamic, gives voice to a pending crisis.

In this way, prayer pictures add a depth and breadth that a pastor won't find in a name simply added to the bottom of a list.

Prayer offered up in the moment serves as a window through which an attentive pastor can gauge the health of his or her congregation.

I give thanks for my family.
Love, Stuart.

Stu hasn't always drawn himself into the portrait. This was particularly evident when his brother was very young. Then he began to draw himself back in, to include himself in the portrait. This particular offering shows the health of this family. All those smiles make the pastor want to smile as well.

I pray for my mom. Kathryn

Kathryn's Mom is having such a great day, that Kathryn herself offers up this prayer on her Mom's behalf. In the Book of Common Prayer, a petition is offered, "shield the joyous." That's the essence of Kathryn's prayer.

Anna-Leia has a new brother. You can tell by the expression on her face that she feels pretty good about him. The sun shines on the two of them. Shines on her dog as well.

Anna-Leia has a new brother!

Anna-Leia feels so good, in fact, that she draws Mary and Joseph and the baby Jesus into the family portrait.

Anna-Leia joins the "Holy Family."

This is a wonderful moment in the prayer life of a child. God is immanent and accessible to her. She is as connected to the Holy Family as she is to her own. In fact, she doesn't make much distinction.

Other prayers on other days may reflect a more problematic or mercurial relationship with these new events. Prayer cards, offered routinely, allow a lay or clergy pastor to read the family "barometer" in new and immediate ways.

Children carry their extended families to church with them. The members of your congregation will soon know them by name. You will know their birthdays and anniversaries. Prayers for the extended family reminds us that we are a part of something so much bigger than ourselves, the communion of saints.

I would like to thank God for Grandmas.
Love, Paige.

Paige's love extends far beyond her own grand-mother to encompass a world of grandmothers.

We pray for Opa in the nursing home.
By Grace

Members of the Holy Family congregation talk with Grace about Opa, about the nursing home, about nursing homes in general.

Grandma and Lexi

If a child is not yet writing, a parent or older sibling or friend may write the prayer message on the card.

We pray for our grandma Betty
who is in remission.

Given the opportunity, children can achieve a remarkable sophistication in their understanding of illness. They can pray about it. Write about it. Draw their fears and concerns and hopes.

Prayer and a Ministry of Healing

Children pray for healing. They pray without that fog of self-consciousness which seems to encumber adults.

Daddy on his bike

My Daddy is riding his bike from San Francisco to Los Angeles, starting today. He'll be gone for eight days and I miss him already. He's riding to help make money for people with AIDS so they can find cures and the people with AIDS can get better. There are a lot of people with AIDS so they need lots of people to ride their bikes. I think he's very brave. But I'm not very brave.

As we moved from our prayers through the Confession and Peace to Holy Communion, four cyclists came through the entrance doors, Lexi's dad among them. Their route had brought them south on Highway One right past the church, and these four arrived just in time for Communion. Recalling that moment, the sense of community, the support and love so visible as to be palpable, still brings me to tears. I see Lexi's face as she put the picture together. I hear her cry of joy. I see her fling herself at her father's knees, he in his spandex bicycle shorts and top, his face flushed with exertion and burned from the sun. I can see him remove a glove to receive the bread in one hand, his other arm gathering his wife and all three children in an embrace.

When we allow and insist that our children be given opportunity to exercise their ministries, this is what happens. It is not an accident. Nor is it a one-time occurrence. This child with leukemia attended our pre-school, and found himself at the heart of immeasurable love and generosity and care. The children of the pre-school and the children of the church grew in love and courage and candor and hope.

This seemingly innocuous prayer card opened a window of spontaneous discussion for the gathered community. When Lexi brought it up to me to read, she began to cry, and this is the story as she unfolded it.

A prayer for a suffering child.

For Reflection:

- Pray like this for a period of weeks, using prayer cards and markers.

- What do the "prayer snapshots" show you about the lives of the members of your congregation?

Prayer and Congregational Ministry

Children know what ministry is, and they want to exercise their own. Children at Holy Family serve as acolytes. They also serve on the altar guild, setting up for the main service, cleaning up after it. Claire once said of her altar guild work, "It's my duty." Another child said, "It's how I pray."

Adults are prone to error, I think, when we link our concepts of children and ministry to form "ministry to children." Children, like all of us, have a ministry, both within and without the congregation. Our task as community is to help one another discern our ministry, to encourage our ministry, and to support our ministry.

Take advantage of opportunities to affirm your congregation's children as they begin to grow in ministry. Help them to shape and to form their gifts.

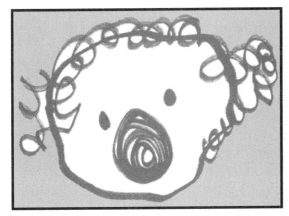

Dear God, thank you for singing.

This child knows the source of his own gift of singing. He is a pianist as well, and understands God as the author of all music. If you were to talk with him, he would tell you about his ministry of music. He sings to make people happy.

We sing for Jusses

This child speaks from her God-centeredness. People in our congregation pay attention to her. They listen. A grandparent once asked her if singing solo, as she had that morning, made her nervous. "Not when I'm singing for God," she said.

Ministry of Ecology

I mentioned once in a sermon, that our word "ecology" is derived from two Greek words: *oikos*, the word for house; and *Logos*, the word for Word or God. When we speak of ecology, we speak of God's house. It's the house that we share with all creation, and maybe it's time to care for God's house in a new way.

The children of Holy Family took this to heart. It was from this sermon that the work of one or two members of the congregation vis à vis the re-planting of San Bruno Mountain in San Mateo County became the focus of community ministry.

The prayers of the children shifted to include all kinds of diverse populations of the world, from general to specific.

Dear God, thank you for nature.
We love you, God.

I pray for all the animals in the world.

We pray for those who have been designated endangered. We pray for the forgotten creatures: panthers, cheetahs and leopards. We pray for the unlovely creatures: snakes, praying mantises, reptiles, snails, and insects.

God bless all creatures of the world,
especially turtles.

Many of our prayers come closer to home. Children, I think, understand "home" in ways that enrich the tapestry. Everything that God has made falls within the embrace of "home."

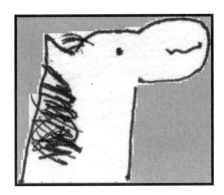

Thank you
for ponies

For all the
Hamsters

When a child offers a prayer for bugs or snakes or any of our unloved creatures, make room for that prayer. "Its been a long time since we've prayed for snakes. Snakes are fascinating creatures."

Ministry of Justice

In a prayer such as this one, you can see a child begin to make connections...earth, sun, flower, grass, self, family, and God. This child is not separate from God's creation. She considers herself an integral part of it.

I love my whole
family and God.

The pastoral flavor of these prayers spills over into the issue of justice. There is a deep sense of justice and integrity reflected in them. The question for the church community is "How do we provide a matrix to foster and nurture this kind of expression of reconciling love?" Look to the prayer life of your children for its prophetic voice. Train your eyes and your hearts to see.

Endangerment is not only an ecological concern, it is a justice concern. Allow the prayers of your children, speaking the prophetic voice, to empower your own. Consider having a conversation and "call to action" whose focus is animals' endangerment.

Bless our animals

Ministry of Prophecy

There are those who make the claim that the children and youth of our congregations are the prophets, that they carry the voice of prophecy.

It is my experience that the prophetic voice of children contains uncommon clarity. Thus says the Lord: Peace is good. Thus says the Lord: Nature is good. Thus says the Lord: Love can work miracles. This has been our experience as we share our life of common prayer.

Can you hear what the children are saying? Can you hear it fresh, as something other than an empty shell of a political promise? Peace.

I pray for the world,
that there is peace.

For Reflection:

- Consider the ways in which your congregation works toward peace.
- Are your goals clear?
- Do your actions for peace correspond to your goals?

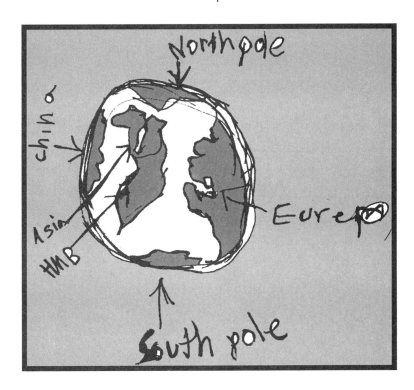

I pray for World Peace
in Vietnam and Boznia.

Love and peace can work miracles!

I pray for all the people in the world,
and for the animals.

For Reflection:

- How can you help your children exercise their ministry of prayer?
- How can you *allow* your children, is perhaps more to the point.
- Can you step aside, and make room for them in the prayer life of your congregation?

I love God.
I love the
whole world.

Every Sunday, every time we gather as a community, we are called into love, called into peace, by our children. They are not talking into the wind. They are the prophets. They are talking to us. Directly. I love God. I love the world. I pray for all the people. I pray for all the animals. I pray for peace.

How hard it has become for those of us who love the language of prayer, who love how the words sound as we string them together like popcorn, who love the history and tradition of their sounds, how hard it has become for us to find the heart of prayer, to find prayer's meaning.

Ministry of Liturgy

The prayer life of a congregation shapes its worship, shapes its mission focus, shapes its conversations and its education. The prayers of children, in their clarity and their artistry, are powerful indicators of the health of mission within a given community of faith.

Given the opportunity, children develop their prayer life around the cycles of the church year in much the same way that adults do.

A Child's Prayer:

"I love you God and Jesus! Merry Christmas!"

God, you been born on
Christmas. I love you so
much that you can come to
my birthday party. Because
I love you.

"Dear God,
Have a good
Palm Sunday."

I, like many of us, I suspect, had learned to pull my punches about Jesus on the cross. "Children aren't ready to hear that part of the story," as though there were a story at all without that part.

This prayer sparked a lively discussion about how God might feel about Palm Sunday. Does God know what's about to happen to Jesus? Is God sad? But is there a moment where God, if God were on earth, would be waving palm branches, too?

Can God be happy and sad at the same time?

A long time ago
it was called
God Friday,
but somewhere along
the line, someone
added the other "O" and made it good.

The prayer life of children often catches adults off balance. When one child, at the age of seven and in total indignation and out-rage, interrupted the Mass to ask about Jesus, "You mean he died?" I didn't know what to do.

I, like many of us, I suspect, had learned to pull my punches about Jesus on the cross. "Children aren't ready to hear that part of the story," as though there were a story at all without that part.

"Yes," was all that I could manage as a response to this boy, and a feeble yes at that.

The next week came the following prayer.

Dear Jesus,
Thanks for
dying for us.

Given the chance, children are quick to make the connections between death and life, and they are comfortable in the expression of their understanding.

God is always with you.

A Child's Prayer

Today is not just a day when the Easter Bunny hides eggs. It is a special day that comes two days after Good Friday, when Jesus rose from the dead. We celebrate this day because of that.

A Child's Prayer

I'm sorry Jesus died.

Now because he lives the moon shines bright.

GOODY.

Ministry of Theology

Not only are our children prophets, they are philosophers and theologians as well. They know the source of all their gifts and they know gratitude.

In a prayer conversation not long ago, children were discussing how your heart grew when you gave it away. They spoke in terms of its size.

"This big?" I asked them. "Does it get this big?"

"No. Bigger."

And they drew pictures that day, before and after pictures, of their hearts growing bigger.

"So...then," I asked, pushing this conversation a little further. "What is your prayer?"

"That we be generous when we grow up, too."

"And what's your prayer for the grown-ups?"

"That you remember what happens to your heart when you give stuff away."

Have you ever noticed that when left to themselves children think deeply about the same subjects adults do? Their conclusions may be different, and "illogical" to adults, but their theology is profound. Allow children their theological voice.

Thank you for our hearts
that make us love. Or
we would always be
mean and grouchy.

I pray for my Guardian Angels and all Angels.

For Reflection:

• Think of a time when you or your family or someone you loved was in danger. Did you have a sense of the divine protection?
• What was that like for you?
• Share this experience with someone else.

Prayer cards offer the opportunity to stop and talk about things. These angels were the core of a prayer conversation about the occasions we have known ourselves as safe in God's love.

When I read this child's card, offering a prayer for all the angels, a man new to our congregation stood up and began to speak of his alcoholism and his process of recovery. He spoke of his sense of safety in the program of Alcoholics Anonymous. He asked the children if they thought there were angels on earth.

Unplanned and unrehearsed, he witnessed to the congregation about those earthly angels he had met in AA.

I pray for
the Good Words
that we speak.
Hello.

A prayer card such as the one to the right offers an opportunity to raise issues of diversity: race, culture, age, gender, and religion.

The prayer below sparked a discussion about the way we talk to one another in school. Adults began to speak of how they talk (and are talked to) at work.

no
to
eggs
are the same.
no two of the
you are
the very same

We are all very different but much the same.
God loves us a lot!

When prayers are personal and immediate, wonderful conversations happen. This prayer, for example, initiated reflections about cultural diversity and faith diversity. Children know the breadth and depth of God's love. They quickly find themselves in tension, however, as they see how that is played out, on the streets, in their schools, even at home.

Prayer as Poetry

A Poem by Heather

The moon looks bright,
The moon that shines.
I love you, God, so much.
I pray you guide me all day long.

A Poem by Raymond

Gods have the feelings of you
They are sad
They are mad.
They are joyful
They are loving
Just like you.
God wears the clothes you wear.
But God is not you.
God is the one in your heart.

Prayer is "Naming the Powers"

Children pray the monsters in their closets and under their beds. Praying their monsters is a way to name them, lift them up, into the light of God. They become part of a child's consciousness, no longer hidden in deep shadow. Children speak them, praying their struggles. Children pray their deepest fears.

For Reflection:

• How might you allow children to pray their doubts and their dark places?
• How might you help them bring God into those places?

The bat cat mom monster

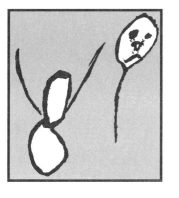

Dear Mr. God.
Why do you make
it so easy for people
to come apart?

Children pray their struggles. Children pray their deepest fears.

The children will tell you, their teacher, or you, their pastor, what parts of their lives are seeking your attention. There is no family barometer more accurate.

The child who drew herself with tears was in church with her Dad and sister that morning for the first time in quite a while. They were able to speak to members of the congregation about the parents' separation.

That prayer and subsequent disclosure marked the beginning of healing for the family which includes the kind of congregational support pastors and educators often only talk about.

Jack's Concluding Prayer

As we conclude our prayer time each Sunday, the whole congregation offers a simple "echo" prayer (the congregation echoes each phrase spoken by the prayer leader) with attendant hand gestures.

Dear God here I am.
Giving thanks for this day.
With Jesus your Son,
I give you this day.
I give you my heart,
and with you I pray.
Your Kingdom will come.
AMEN

I was the prayer leader not too long ago, and as I led this concluding prayer, a young child, two and a half years old, placed himself directly in front of me, planted his feet wide, and proceeded to do what I was doing.

As we moved from gesture to gesture, speaking each phrase, he watched and then copied with an intensity that staggered me.

Time suspended, we moved as though in slow motion.

Soon there were only two people in the room, he and I, locked in a prayer dance as powerful and as profound as anything I've ever experienced.

Something happens corporately, when a prayer carried in the heart of one person, a child or an adult, is offered into the body. The corporate heart is quickened. The embrace widens. Conversations are initiated. Candor is valued. Conversion happens.

Let your children pray with you. Make room for them to exercise their ministry of prayer. It will transform your congregation.

Give Me a New Heart, O God

Chapter Five

My Lan's Story

The first time I heard My Lan's laughter, she was coming up the stairs of the church office, being carried on the back of her fiancé, Richard. The stairs were steep, and so the two of them were struggling. The more precarious their balance, the more joyfully My Lan seemed to laugh. She was recovering from reconstructive surgery on both feet, undertaken to correct the damage inflicted upon her as an adolescent during the Vietnam War. My Lan was a victim of war, both physically and spiritually.

She and Richard and I had arranged to meet to discuss their upcoming wedding. During the course of the first discussion, Richard indicated his strong desire to receive Holy Communion at the wedding.

"No," said My Lan.

"It will be important to the people who come," Richard told her.

"No," said My Lan.

"It will be important to me," he said.

"No."

The next time we met, My Lan was walking with canes.

"I have something to tell you," she said in her soft voice. "I cannot have Communion because I have not made confession for thirty-one years. I do not want Holy Communion because it has too much pain."

As her story unfolded, I learned that My Lan had been raised in the Roman Catholic Church. She took her First Communion at the age of seven, was confirmed at twelve.

But by the time she was thirteen, My Lan's parents had both been killed, and My Lan was responsible for the lives of her five sib-

For Reflection:

- The burdens that we carry in our hearts may or may not come immediately to the surface.
- Are there burdens in your own life that you have carried for a long time?

lings. She learned to steal. She stole food, clothing, other things to sell or trade. She stole cigarettes and exchanged them for seeds.

Her priest refused her Communion until she had confessed her sins. She could not in good faith promise her priest an amendment of life that required that she stop stealing. She needed to feed her family.

"Thirty-one years," she said. "I can't figure this out."

Over the next few weeks, we figured it out together. My Lan did make confession, but it was not the stealing that she confessed, because her sinfulness did not lie in the act of stealing. The fact that My Lan was forced to steal in order to provide physical sustenance for herself and her siblings was a reflection of something far greater, something far more evil—the sins of injustice, of violence, aggression, and greed. Those were not her sins.

What My Lan did confess was her alienation from God and from her faith community. She and Richard did offer and receive Holy Communion at their wedding.

After this experience, I began to pay attention to the centrality of confession in one's spiritual life and journey. I began to pay attention to the centrality of confession in the lives of children.

The Centrality of Confession

I asked Toby, fourteen, and Kelsey, thirteen, how they were doing.

"Not too good," they told me. "Somebody called the cops on us last night." Piece by piece, the story came out. They had been throwing oranges at cars. "But we weren't trying to hit them."

But Kelsey hit one. "By mistake," they assured me.

"And the guy in the car wasn't even mad. It was some woman sitting on her porch. It wasn't even her business. She's the one who called the cops."

Kelsey ran. The police caught Toby and made him tell them who the other kid was. They knocked on Kelsey's door and told his dad. Then Kelsey's dad told Toby's dad.

And as they told me the story, something became very clear. I was not dragging this story out of them, Toby and Kelsey were wanting to tell it. They needed to tell it. And they needed someone to call them into account. I asked them what they thought they ought to do.

"Well, we can't apologize to the guy in the car we hit with the orange. We don't know who he was or where he lives."

"What about the woman sitting on the porch?"

"Her! No way! She wasn't even in it!"

"No, she wasn't in it, but next time it might be her car with her in it. That orange might go right through her windshield."

Toby and Kelsey agreed to apologize to the woman who was sitting on her porch when they threw the orange and hit the car.

The centrality of confession.

I know when a child has something to confess. She meets me at the door to my office, or even halfway along the sidewalk, so great is the need to release her heart from her burden.

For Reflection:

- An ethical dilemma is not always a choice between something that is right and something that is wrong. Often we are required to choose between something that is wrong and something else that is wrong.
- Have you ever found yourself in such a situation?
- What did you choose?

Things Done and Left Undone

Often the words in our prayer books become rote, and the action meaningless. Frequently there is no naming of the sin(s), no reflection upon either the sin or the possibility of restoration.

Children bring an immediacy to the Rite of Confession, an immediacy and a freshness of perspective. Children take this moment in the worship service seriously.

Some form of confession is standard practice on most worship occasions. Some denominations require individual confession on a regular basis. Others offer a general confession which is prayed corporately on a given day of worship, with penitents confessing, in a non-specific way, things done and left undone.

For Reflection:

How might we design a form of confession in such a way that all congregants, adults and children alike, can enter in?

The question we need to ask of the rite itself is the same question we ask of each piece of our worship service, as we open it up to the full participation of children: How might we design a form of confession in such a way that all congregants, adults and children alike, can enter in?

My image is one of cracking open, as in cracking open the shell of a walnut or pecan. How do you crack open a form so that all people may taste the meat of it?

And then we have to ask a further question. What is it of our outward behavior that we confess that reflects a greater sickness in our soul?

Confession Stones

Never underestimate the power of dreams. I dreamed one night of stones—small, smooth stones—and the seed of a Rite of Confession was planted.

I set the children upon a task. "Gather stones from the beach, from your yard, from your favorite places. Bring them to me."

That task soon blossomed. Families began to gather what we named "pilgrimage stones," from vacations, business trips, walks on the beach. Children brought them back from various places, eager to add them to our pool. The congregation now has stones from the Canadian Yukon and the Arctic Circle. From London, Nova Scotia, and Southern Ohio.

The stones are kept in what we named Confession Stone Holders, small clay pots the older children made, which have been attached to the backs of our pews. Each ceramic pot is filled with stones, and at the time of confession, we ask each person in the congregation to take one.

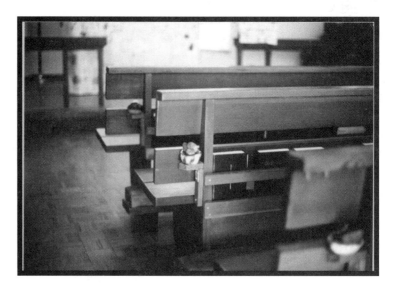

Confession Stone Holders are attached to the backs
of the pews and filled with stones.

Confession Meditation

The following meditation forms the foundation for Holy Family's confession of sin. If you use something like this, you don't have to do the meditation itself every week, just the confession. I would suggest you do meditation often enough that the people in the congregation remember it, and new people are introduced to it.

I say this because I know of several congregations who have adopted the rite without introducing its theology. When this happens, the confession quickly becomes disconnected and ultimately meaningless.

It is not necessary that a priest lead this meditation. Lay people of any age are welcome to do it. The Holy Family congregation often does it as an interactive conversation.

The leader might begin, "Let's talk about Moses in the desert, when he struck the rock. What happened?"

Meditation: The Rock, the Promise, and the Christ

Many thousands of years ago, the people of God lived as slaves in Egypt under the harsh rule of the Egyptian kings. The slaves cried out to God, and God heard their cries. God called Moses to lead the people out of slavery into freedom.

Moses led them across the raging waters of the Red Sea, and into the desert, where they continued a sojourn begun long ago by their ancestors Abraham and Sarah.

Before God sent the manna from the heavens, there was no food in the desert and the people were hungry. They were angry and they pointed their rage toward Moses. You should have left us in Egypt. At least we had plenty to eat. Perhaps that was fact, perhaps only a fantasy.

There was nothing to drink in the desert. The people were thirsty. God said to Moses, "Hit this rock with your staff." Moses did what God had instructed, and water poured forth. And he called that rock Meribah because of the people's disbelief.

The Rock at Meribah became a source of water in a barren and thirsty land.

It came Joshua's turn to lead the people of God, through the waters of the Jordan on their journey to the Promised Land. As in the days of long before, the swollen waters dried up under the hand of God, and the people of Israel crossed safely.

Joshua ordered them to gather twelve stones from the Jordan, and they did, carrying them with them until they made camp at Gilgal.

Joshua told his people, "In the days to come, when your descendants ask their fathers and mothers what these stones mean, you shall explain that the Jordan was dry when Israel crossed over, and that the Lord your God dried up the waters of the Jordan in front of you until you had gone across, just as the Lord your God did at the Red Sea when he dried it up for us until we had crossed."

The rocks across the Jordan became the pathway to the Promised Land.

Thousands of years later Jesus of Nazareth walked the towns and villages of Palestine, preaching, teaching, healing the sick, and casting out demons. One day he stepped down into the river, into the hands of his cousin, John, and was baptized by John in the waters of the Jordan. The heavens opened and a dove descended, bearing this message: "You are my beloved child."

Thirty years would pass. And it came to Paul, preaching to the church at Corinth, "You should understand, my brothers and sisters, that our ancestors were all under the pillar of cloud, and all of them passed through the Red Sea; they all ate the same supernatural food, and all drank the same supernatural drink; I mean they all drank from the supernatural rock that accompanied their travels, and that rock was Christ."

That rock was the Christ.

The Rite of Confession

Following the Prayers of the People, I hold up a stone.

"What's this," I ask? I am expecting a response, and I am rarely disappointed.

"It's a confession stone."

"What's it for?" Again, a response is usually quick to come.

"It's to give your broken heart to God."

Those were the words of a child when he was four years old. I had never used those words as any kind of explanation.

The responses are never rote. The children at Holy Family Church have learned that there is no "right" answer.

A Child's Comment:
Nick, age six, says, "Confession makes me feel like I'm with God."

Other Comments:
Maria, age fifty-three, says, "the rock symbolizes the weight of things done and left undone by me. It's the weight of the rock that matters to me. I usually choose a big one."
Laura, who is twenty-three says, "I like the confession stones as symbols. Holding something in my hand makes the things I was thinking about seem more real. I feel like I am getting rid of things when the stones are washed, It is easy to focus on my confession when I am holding a rock. It's more personal. More real. I do my confession and I don't have to explain it. I like it that everyone's stones are washed at the same time. I get a community feeling, like everyone gets fixed together. It's a community experience."

I hold up my own stone. I ask each family or each person or each group of friends to hold onto a stone. And then I tell them this:

This rock, our source of Living Water, becomes the pathway to the Promised Land, the Christ.

Take this rock. Hold onto it. Share it with your neighbor if that seems appropriate.

Hold onto it. Think about the things you have done this week that you wish you hadn't.

Think about the things you didn't do that you wish you had done.

We call these, "things done and left undone."

Lift those burdens, your sins, off your hearts and lay them on the stones. Let the stones carry them.

Source of Living Water, our Pathway to the Promised Land, the Christ, let the stones carry our sins.

Say this after me:

God of Mercy
This week, we have done things against you,
and against each other.
We have harmed the planet and its creatures.
We are sorry.
We are truly sorry.
And we ask your forgiveness.
Help us walk in the way of your love.

This is an adapted version of the General Confession found in the Book of Common Prayer.

The children know what this is about. They go to their families and they talk about the difficulties of their week. And the parents talk to their children. And friends talk to friends.

The same four-year-old who spoke of giving his broken heart to God, once asked forgiveness for being so angry at himself. Another suggested to her mother that her mother confess something she'd done during the course of the week.

The children in the congregation then collect the stones. Picture a dozen or more children walking through the congregation, using their T-shirts, or pockets or hands as containers for the stones. Everybody gathers. It's a wonderful moment, gathering in the burdens and sins of the people in order to give them up to God.

While the children move through the pews, the rest of the congregation sings a piece of music. "A New Heart" by Eric Law is one that works well and can be sung in parts. Another is "Change our Hearts" (refrain only) from the *Gather Hymnal* (GIA Publications, Inc. Chicago).

Choose a song or a refrain that is repeatable, and sing it for the time it takes to bring all the stones to the front.

Once the children have brought the stones forward, they transfer them into a large stainless steel bowl that the leader holds.

Consider other possibilities. For example, during the season of Lent, process to the baptismal font and place the stones in the bowl. The ritual, accomplished in this way, makes a powerful connection between the rite of self-emptying and penitence and the spiritual cleansing action of Baptism.

The children then pour water over the stones as the priest concludes with words of absolution. This is one example:

> Holy God, you have heard the hearts of your people. Wash us clean from our sins as you wash us clean in our Baptism. Have mercy on us. Forgive us. Keep us in eternal life.

Adapt the Form to Specific Occasions

The Rite of Confession, as described above, is infinitely adaptable. If you are celebrating Earth Day, for example, you might add specific language concerning the harm we have done to the planet and her creatures. On the first Sunday after Easter, when many churches hear the story of Doubting Thomas, add language concerning the confession of doubt. If you celebrate the Feast of the Annunciation, add language concerning those times we have failed to say yes to the seed of God.

Charting a Course for Children and the Church

During the closing liturgy of the national Episcopal Church's conference, "Charting a Course for Children in the Church," held at Camp Allen, Texas, October 1998, we used the following meditation:

> As you hold these stones in your hands, consider your own journey through the desert lands. The hot dry places where—to your mind—there is no water to be found. Consider the barren wilderness and hear your own voice of complaint. Moses should have left us as slaves in Egypt. At least we had water to drink.
>
> Consider the pockets where your heart is hardened, perhaps by a future not yet revealed, perhaps by fear or anxiety, perhaps by failure. Put that hardness onto these stones. Let these stones carry what is broken and in need of restoration.
>
> As you hold these stones in your hands, consider the opportunities you haven't acknowledged, the things you've left undone, untried, the life unexamined. Lift those things from your hearts and let the stones carry them.

Following the meditation, the priest leads the people in confession and the rite continues as outlined above. On that occasion, we placed our stones in the baptismal font.

As you explore the meaning and significance of the stones in the life of your community, you needn't limit yourselves to the metaphors suggested here: source of Living Water; God's promise; the Christ.

Consider Peter, Cephas, as the Rock, when Jesus says to him, "On this Rock I will build my church."

Consider the stones as signs of your own corporate journey. They are rich in symbolism, limited only by the breadth of our imaginations.

The Community of the Bathtized

Chapter Six

An Eight-Year-Old's Question

The occasion of my first Baptism was pretty standard for families whose church backgrounds are more social than religious. My mother contacted our minister to tell him it was probably time to "do" the first two babies, and apparently he agreed. I was an infant, and have no memory of that moment.

So it is an occasion of surprise and privilege for me when the conversation about Baptism is initiated by a child.

One Sunday morning an eight-year-old in our congregation approached me. "Can I be bathtized?" she asked.

"Of course," I told her. "Of course," and I smiled, knowing absolutely that the thrust of her next question would once again reflect my own sense of inadequacy.

"What does it mean, bathtized?"

How do you tell her what it means, this ancient, sacred ritual that announces itself as an occasion for family to gather at a time other than Thanksgiving or Christmas, an occasion for the naming of an additional set of parents, an occasion for dressing up, an occasion for a celebration. An occasion that has something to do not only with you, but with you and God. An occasion that—if you announce it to the world, as an eight-year-old is likely to do—you will be met with looks of incomprehension, greeted as an oddity...the world's eyes, perhaps, rolled skyward.

How do you tell an eight-year-old? You might, as a colleague suggests, ask what it means to her. What is it that she has seen or heard that has planted this sacred seed in her own soul?

For some children, it is question of fact.

"I want to be an acolyte and you told me I had to be baptized first."

"My friends are baptized."
"I want something special with God."
"I want Melissa's mom to be my mom, too."
Or...you might tell a story.

What Are Our Stories?

As I said, my first Baptism was nothing out of the ordinary. It's my second Baptism that I remember.

My mother packed special dresses for me and for my big sister, Nancy. We were four and six. Off we went to Huntington, West Virginia, to be baptized in my great-grandparents' church, dunked by a man who was not my minister. I was ecstatic, and upon my return, as the legend goes, I jumped out of the station wagon, flung myself at my grandmother's knees and told her, "I was natized, Gram. I was natized. They poured water all over my head and they natized me."

Whatever it was that had happened to me, and however I understood it, I remember it as a highly significant and formative moment of my life. I was special. I was special because I got to take a trip, and I was special with God.

During my years as a seminarian, I pretty well unlearned everything I knew about the glorious and powerful experience itself so that I could concentrate on the doctrine and tradition of Baptism. I find that not uncommon. I also find it sad.

I learned many things. I learned that the church of my denomination didn't do private Baptisms any more; Baptism had become a corporate event. I learned that the Episcopal Church had designated four days over the course of the liturgical year as appropriate for Baptisms. And I learned that we don't do Baptisms during the season of Lent because baptismal theology is an Easter theology, and requires the celebration of the Resurrection.

During my second year in seminary, my brother asked me to be the godmother of his four-year-old-daughter, who was to be baptized in my grandmother's church, the same grandmother whose knees I had grasped in ecstasy some forty years before.

My mother was arguing for a private Baptism.

"That's how we did all of you," she said. "Besides, we don't know these people in your grandmother's church, and they certainly don't know us. Or care, for that matter."

I puffed myself up with all the weight of my learning that I could gather.

"We don't baptize like that any more." I wielded an authority that only a seminarian can muster. "Baptism is a community occasion and needs to be celebrated by the community."

No one paid me the least attention. Why should they? After all, wasn't this just Carol, who sucked her thumb well into the seventh grade?

They decided to ask the minister.

"We'd like to do the Baptism privately," my mother informed him, on her next visit.

For Reflection:

- What do you remember of your Baptism?

- What family legends, if any, surround the occasion of your Baptism?

- Whether or not you chose or were given a new name at your Baptism, what significance does your name carry for you?

"Oh, we don't do it like that anymore. Baptisms are celebrations for the community."

Didn't I feel righteous!

But Baptism isn't about righteousness. It isn't about rubric. Or, if it is about rubric, then it has to be a rubric that yields to the pastoral concerns of any given situation. Because Baptism is about relationship. It's about belonging. It's about joy and surrender. It's about covenant and commitment.

Less than three years after my prideful righteousness concerning the Baptism of my goddaughter, I was making plans to baptize three children, in the privacy of their own home.

The parents had requested it. The youngest of the three was autistic, and the family was very uncomfortable in public situations. Their love of God and the desire of the parents to baptize their children was in direct conflict with their fear and despair in public outings.

As we made the decision to baptize the children at home, the clericalism of my own world view began to unravel to allow the Spirit room to maneuver. The "I" in the baptismal formula of my own denomination, "I baptize you in the name of the Father," shifted to "we." That single word has altered my experience of community forever.

I happened to mention the upcoming private Baptism to a seminarian who was laid up in the hospital with a bad back. "You can't baptize them privately," he told me with an authority that was embarrassingly familiar. "Baptism is a community occasion."

A Question of Priorities

What does Baptism mean to the person desiring it? Reflection on that question determines the process and the particulars of the occasion.

What matters? That's the question that drives the decision making around a Baptism. It's the same question that drives the decision making around any service of worship.

What matters?

What matters the most? And to ask that takes us back to the initial questions: What is the experience of Baptism? How do we know ourselves as reborn? How do we know ourselves as the Body of Christ?

Maybe what matters the most to the person desiring to be baptized is that she anchor herself in an ancient tradition by walking the catechumenate path of the early church. Her preparation and study might take a year, even longer.

Maybe what matters the most is the timing. The grandparents have arranged their visit for late March, which coincides with the third Sunday of Lent. Where is the priority when the needs of the family bump up against a tradition that argues against Lenten Baptisms?

Maybe what matters the most is a connectedness to the environment. Maybe a child would ask to be baptized on the beach, or in a redwood forest, or a mountain top.

Maybe what matters the most is belonging.

For Reflection:

- Bring to mind an occasion of Baptism in your own congregation.
- How was that experience for you?
- What does it mean to you to be part of the baptizing community?

For Reflection:

Where is the priority when the pastoral needs of the family bump up against the liturgical tradition?

"Will you strive for justice and peace among all people, and respect the dignity of every human being?" BCP, 305.

Will You Strive For Justice?

Full inclusion of all members in the worshiping body of the church is an issue of justice, and justice is the foundation of our baptismal covenant. Children aren't in church because of the generosity of a congregation's heart. Children are in church because they're meant to be there. Nowhere is this stated more clearly than in our baptismal theology.

The questions put to the community, in one form or another, are these:

"Will you strive for justice and peace among all people?" And, "Will you who witness these vows do all in your power to support these persons in their life in Christ?"

The full inclusion of children and youth in such a way as to allow them participation in the decisions affecting their lives—family, environment, education, economics, church—is an issue of justice.

Meaning and Structure

For those denominations who work from a given order of worship, the question of meaning must engage the prescribed structure. Among Episcopalians and Lutherans, for example, the baptismal forms are offered in their books of common worship. The framework is similar. So the questions of the baptismal liturgy itself are determined by the pastoral needs of the family.

Presentation

Consider the words, "We present this child to receive the sacrament of Baptism."

Who is this child? Who is his family?

The presentation of an infant or an older child for Baptism is a powerful occasion for deepening that family's connection to the community.

It's a time to share with the congregation the part of the family's journey that brought them to this place at this time. It's an opportunity to tell the people gathered who this child is, perhaps by the story of his name. Is he named after a relative? A figure in history? How does this child's name reflect the deep desire and integrity of the family's heart? The name Erin, for example, from Irene means peace, and it was clearly a factor in the parents' decision to so name their child.

The presentation is a time to introduce godparents, who may or may not be members of the congregation.

It's a time for a family to say to the congregation, and the congregation to say back, we are a part of you.

The Prayers

Pray your deep hopes and yearnings for this child being baptized. Write a poem.

At Holy Family Church, I asked that the community—parents, godparents, siblings, friends, and members of the congregation—write the prayers for those being baptized.

"Pray your deep hopes and yearnings for this child," I tell people. "Write a poem. Consider it a spiritual exercise of your own, to discover more about your relationship to this child, to discover deeper meaning of this moment."

It is a profound moment of intimate connection for a congregation, to hear and to offer prayers for the one being baptized. The godparents of Lauren and Ben offered this prayer:

We thank you God:
for the life and love you have given Lauren and Ben:
for blessing them with loving and nurturing parents and
        grandparents:
for the Holy Family Community which helps them grow
        closer to you and to others.
We ask you to bless them
with awareness of your great love for them;
with spirits that rejoice in your creation;
with actions for others that witness your love;
with laughter, music, dance, and love of life;
with a spirit of forgiveness for self and others;
with desire to know you better, to hear your voice, and
        to be your friend.

Here is the prayer offered by their parents:

Dear Lord,
We thank you for your many blessings and especially
        these children, Lauren and Ben.
We now humbly ask that as they learn and grow and go
        into your world that you will protect them from
        harm.
Give them wisdom and discernment.
For Ben we ask that he grow to feel comfortable sharing
        himself and his talents.
For Lauren we ask that she learn to use her gifts wisely
        and with compassion for others.
Give Ben and Lauren your loving comfort and guide them
        to a place of light, peace and joy.

Lauren herself (age seven) offered this prayer

Dear God,
Put your blessing
upon us.

I pray
that me and
my brother
have a good life.

Ben (age two and a half)

We thank you
God for giving us
this bread. We thank
you for blessing our
family.

Water Dance by Thomas Locker provides a strong foundation for any conversation with children about water.

About the Water

Water is central in baptismal preparation for anyone, and a source of power and understanding for children. Children know about water. They know that water cleanses, it cools, it quenches thirst. Water provides a home for whales and dolphins. It makes things grow. It's the substance of our tears. They know these things, and they want to let you know they know.

The threads between water and community, water and God, water and self are already at their work of making connection.

If you are wanting to have a conversation with a child about water, take a look at the book *Water Dance* by Ben Locker. Using simple language and powerful paintings, the book tells of the connectedness of all life, the cycles of all life, using living water as its source.

> Some people say I am one thing.
> Others say that I am many.
> Ever since the world began
> I have been moving in endless circles.
> Sometimes I fall from the sky.
> I am the rain.

From rain to mountain stream, to waterfall, to lake, Locker moves the cycle, and he continues.

> I wind through the broad golden valleys
> joined by streams,
> joined by creeks, I grow ever wider,
> broader, deeper.
> I am the River.

Then the sea, then mist and cloud, thunderhead, storm, and rainbow. Until finally,

> I am one thing
> I am many things.
> I am water.
> This is my dance through our world.

It is a story of mystery and awe, great silences, great thunderous power, a story of life and connectedness, a story of wholeness and movement, of cycles begun and completed.

It works gloriously as a foundation for baptismal instruction, particularly with children.

If it's an infant being baptized, who has older siblings, or if it's a child, I ask their help in composing the prayer over the water. We write the prayer over the water together. Because children know so much about water, this is an exercise that challenges them to make deeper connections, to put ideas and concepts together in new ways.

The prayer over the water that two brothers, aged eleven and seven, helped adapt for their Baptisms looks like this:

Holy God, we thank you for your gift of water. We are ninety-seven percent water. Maybe more. Without it we are nothing. It's the water of our bodies. It's the water of our oceans and rivers and lakes and streams and storms.

In the beginning, the Holy Spirit of God breathed over the water and gave it life. Through it you led your children of Israel out of slavery into freedom.

It's the water with which we wash and make ourselves clean. This water of Baptism makes us clean inside, makes us clean in our hearts. In it, your child Jesus was baptized by his cousin John.

Thank you God, for the water of Baptism. In it we share in the death of Christ. It's the water of our tears, the water of our pain and our brokenness. Through it we are born a new time into a life lived in you.

Bless this water, O God. Make it holy water for these children, and for all who are baptized in the name of Jesus.

We Welcome You

Following the Baptism, the community welcomes its newest member, often by a specified prayer. The children of our community design and construct the welcome for each new child. They take each of the four charges—as they appear in the Book of Common Prayer—and draw illustrations.

Below is an example of a welcome for the newly baptized, designed and illustrated by the children of Holy Family Church.

"We welcome you into the household of God. Confess the faith of Christ crucified, proclaim his resurrection, and share with us in his eternal priesthood." BCP, 308.

More Baptismal Artwork

Have your children design and make a baptismal bowl. Use the colors of the sea and baptismal symbols. We asked the children to imprint their hands inside and outside into the clay. We scalloped the rim of the bowl with a shell.

Once we realized that we had such a treasure in our midst, we commissioned a craftsman to fashion an iron stand that matches the stand of our Paschal Candle.

Then we designed the banner which we use in procession at every Baptism. At the top is a scallop shell, dressed in silver and gold glitter, from which cascades a waterfall of children's hands. In the lower right corner, in flaming red, are the gifts of the Spirit, some of them anyway:

Joy, friendship, sensitivity, happiness, peace, caring, hope, love...

For Reflection:

- The children of Holy Family have named the gifts of the Spirit: joy, friendship, sensitivity, happiness, peace, caring, hope, and love.
- What gifts of the Spirit might your children add to the list?

The Search for Meaning

Fill your baptismal services with opportunities to experience the joy and wonder of the sacred, to deepen the sense of community, and to foster a vision of the Kingdom of God. Baptism is not so much about instruction. It's about conversion and renewal. In 1994, John Westerhoff, in a seminar on preaching at the College of Preachers, observed that the task of congregations is to raise up dreamers and lovers and children of vision.

Everything you can do, to move to the heart of this ancient and sacred tradition, is work that deepens the soul's yearning and journey to God.

Come to the Table

What Stories Can You Tell?

I was thirteen years old the day of my First Communion, that day coinciding with the day of my confirmation. It was also the Sunday that my family and I returned from spring break. We'd been skiing for a week, and I intended to come home with a tan. The fact that I had red hair and fair freckled skin didn't bother me because I had discovered Man Tan. Rub it on. Instant tan.

The problem was, I had neglected to wash it off my hands. The lotion colored my palms with sickly orange blotches. I decided to wear my mother's white gloves to the altar rail, but my bishop would not serve me the host until I had removed at least one glove. To my embarrassment, he and my mother negotiated that decision as though I had no ears.

I received Communion that day because it was my confirmation day. But I didn't go to the altar again for months, and many years had passed before I could receive Communion without remembering the shame and humiliation of my first encounter with the Body of Christ.

I don't think one's First Communion is intended to be such an isolating experience. But neither was my experience an isolated one.

In most congregations, particularly congregations of liturgical churches whose worship derives from the ancient forms, we hear a familiar voice. "I don't want my child to receive Communion until she understands what it means."

It's a great irony, I think, that even of the more progressive congregations, children usually do not join the eucharistic celebration until some designated moment...an usher sneaks out of the eucharistic prayer at the moment of the elevation of the host, or the introduction

In his address at a recent conference, "Living the Children's Charter: Transforming Lives," (Syracuse, New York, 2000), the Rev. Joe Russell reminds us that Holy Eucharist is the primary formation experience for children and adults alike. "This is where we live the dream of the Kingdom," he said.

A child who is not invited to participate in the preparation for the eucharistic feast will not likely know what the Body and Blood of Christ are about. How could she? For those who wish their children to gain an understanding of the sacraments, separating those children from the preparation for the sacramental feast is self-defeating.

to the Lord's Prayer, and a small bell rings down some hollow corridor, summoning back those who have been removed from the celebrating community during virtually the entire service, for the sake of quiet and order and coloring book pictures of Jesus.

Our children historically have been disconnected from the worshiping community for the bulk of the service, certainly, for the offertory and eucharistic prayers, but most likely from the prayers of the community and the corporate confession as well.

In his address at a recent conference, "Living the Children's Charter: Transforming Lives," (Syracuse, New York, 2000) the Rev. Joe Russell reminded us that Holy Eucharist is the primary formation experience for children and adults alike. "This is where we live the dream of the Kingdom," he said.

It seems to me that a child who is not invited to participate in the preparation for the eucharistic feast will not likely know what the Body and Blood of Christ are about. How could he? For those who wish their children to gain an understanding of the sacraments, separating those children from the preparation for the sacramental feast is self-defeating.

People say to me, "But the children are preparing for Communion out there. They're telling stories of Jesus. They're saying prayers. Sitting around their altar. Just like the adults."

Just like the adults. Maybe so. But they are doing it apart from their own worshiping community. Similarly, the adults are preparing for Communion, but they are not doing it in such a way that includes their children.

Joseph's parents chose to enroll him in a First Communion class when he had just turned seven. We coincided Joseph's First Communion with the bishop's visitation. We were all very excited. The problem? Joseph's First Communion class ended the week prior to the bishop's visit, so there was one Sunday when Joseph was neither in class, nor taking Communion. Joseph was nowhere, and he was the first to recognize it.

As the other children received Communion, Joseph, experiencing the isolation of his particular limbo status—"graduate" and non-communicant—began to cry. Not just cry, he sobbed. Joseph was inconsolable. I was much too late in my recognition of the problem. I couldn't fix it for him. The damage was done.

Think, for a minute, about being seven years old. There is an extraordinary gift for you. You've been preparing for it. Learning about it. Getting excited. It's time. Everybody is sharing this gift. Everybody but you.

It is not fair. It hurts. You are inconsolable.

Think about distributing the bread to child after child after child, but not to Joseph. Why are you withholding the sacrament from this child. Because he doesn't understand? No, he knows everything he needs to at that moment about that gift.

I have not held a First Communion class since that time. I have offered instead a class called, "The Next Communion." It's a class that any child may join and rejoin at any time.

And our children are in church from the opening acclamation until after they have received Communion. What the adults do liturgically, the children do, and they do it together.

We are discovering that any child who is a welcome and regular participant in our Sunday worship, knows the meaning of the eucharistic meal as early as two years old, certainly by two and a half.

The world opened right up for Tom, the day he left his father's over-the-shoulder pouch and learned to walk without falling. He was not shy. He toured the sanctuary during Sunday worship, visiting people, making new friends. Some had smiles, some didn't. Tom loved water, particularly as he poured it out of any container he could find onto the floor.

For a year Tom kept his "designated teen" on the run. He was everywhere. The terror of the Altar Guild. And then one day, seemingly from one Sunday to the next, Tom turned two and a half, and he began to pay attention. Offering prayers, insinuating his body into whatever gaps he could find among the bigger children to attach himself to my person as I read those prayers.

Now he is the first child to reach the altar, only a heartbeat behind the gifts as they are offered. Recently Tom returned to me after I had given him bread. I thought he wanted more, so I offered it. He shook his head. "I can't find the blood of Christ," he whispered. The chalice bearer had moved away from the altar and Tom, at something less than two feet tall, couldn't see him.

Tom is no anomaly. Any child, given the opportunity to participate, can engage the eucharistic liturgy at an astonishingly sophisticated level.

Let's Face It

None of our eucharistic prayers can hold a child's attention. None of them. They are not designed to, and here is where the conversation gets bumpy. I hear frequently, "Children are welcome. Teens are welcome....If they are quiet....If they worship like we do. And don't expect us to change our liturgy." Which is another way of saying that children are not welcome.

If your children are present throughout your Sunday worship, you will have to make some radical changes. One of the biggest challenges is what the Episcopal Church calls the Prayer of Great Thanksgiving, the prayer offered by the priest to consecrate the bread and wine for Communion. Some of the more astute of the Holy Family children refer to it as "the prayer of words."

Rubem Alves, a psychiatrist and theologian, writes:

Silence is the space where words come to life and begin to move. Once they existed because we uttered them. They depended on our will to think, to speak, to write: tame birds in our cages. But in silence a metamorphosis occurs. They become wild, free. They take the initiative. And we can only see and hear. They come to us from beyond. And we find ourselves in another world the beginning of which is the Word. A world we had not visited before. No, maybe we visited it....Maybe we were born in it...but it was forgotten....

The Poet, the Warrior, the Prophet (SCM Press, London, 1990, 30)

Any child, given the opportunity to participate, can engage the eucharistic liturgy at an astonishingly sophisticated level.

Consider pairing up teens with toddlers. Work with the teens until they understand that their task is to help the toddlers to focus on the action of the worship. They are to help them pay attention.

On the day we kicked off our family worship, we invited an Episcopal priest, the Rev. Skip Fotch, to celebrate with us. Skip is a certified clown with a clown ministry in the Diocese of California. His celebration was wordless, a eucharistic dance. His gestures took on the pain and the shame of the broken body, his broken heart poured out. During this wordless prayer, the children did not make a sound. They watched. They moved with the same gestures. They reached for the bread, They fed each other. They fed their families.

Some sixty families attended that service. Many of the adults confessed after the service that this was the first time they had understood the Great Thanksgiving.

The Question of Tradition

As leaders of worship in liturgical churches, we are reluctant to alter either the language or the forms found in our prayer books. Adapt the prayer book rite to meet the needs of a congregation? How dare we? Under what circumstances? How much can we change? If we don't use the right words, is the bread really consecrated?

Think about this. If our liturgies don't express the deepest yearnings of our hearts, if they do not draw us deeper into praise and adoration of the One who creates us and renews us, if the words themselves become obstacles to the devotional needs of a community, then how do we justify our insistence upon their inalterability? This is true for all members of the community, not just the children.

If it is true, and I believe that it is, that all members of the worshiping community have legitimate and urgent claim on what Sunday morning worship (or Friday worship, or Saturday worship) looks like, then the rites must reflect the devotional needs of the entire worshiping congregation, including its children. How do we worship together is the question. How do we break open the Word of God so that it speaks to each of us? How do we come to the table in such a way that the table compels us, together? The operative word is "together."

The traditional logic, however, probably looks something like this. If the children cannot participate appropriately in worship with the adult congregation, then the children need to be segregated. But this is adult-centered logic. And it is not good theology. If the children cannot participate appropriately in worship with the adult congregation, then adapt, develop, or otherwise alter the liturgies until they can.

The worshiping community is misshapen without its young people. And not just without their physical presence, but without their voices, their forms of praise, their joy, their prayer, their prophecy.

Every encounter with a child in worship changes the face of the worshiping community. This is a good thing, not something to be feared.

The process is evolutionary, the tradition itself evolving to deepen the spiritual connectedness of its members. The forms that constrain our rich tradition need to yield to the inevitable and glorious process of evolution.

"Justice shall be the band around his waist, and faithfulness a belt upon his hips. Then the wolf shall be a guest of the lamb, and the leopard shall lie down with the kid; the calf and the young lion shall browse together with a little child to guide them."
Isaiah 11:5–6

The Evolutionary Process

Make room for your children in church. Or, better still, put it another way. Make room for the adults in child-led worship. Help the adults reclaim their childhood, as children of God. Help them discover the renewal of spirit as children do, in their every encounter with God.

This is not about turning our churches over to our children. This is about spiritual and liturgical renewal. This is about communities at worship together, in praise and adoration of God. This is about full inclusion. This is about justice.

This is about coming to the table, together.

Once the commitment is made to help the children understand the eucharistic preparation, the rest begins to unfold itself, and according to your community and its needs.

Children will want to help set the table. Weave them into the Altar Guild.

Invite the children to the altar at Communion, even the youngest.

If you're the presider at the Communion, let yourself experience the power of ten or twenty pairs of small hands sharing the celebration.

Train your youth to be chalice bearers.

Do this one time. Do this once a month. Maybe someday you'll do it every Sunday.

Once you begin, you start to see what's important.

One Sunday, a fight broke out between two sisters. The older one pulled the hair of the younger, and it hurt. Renee began to cry. She crouched down behind the altar, shaking with anger, probably, as well as hurt. She refused the host when I offered it to her.

I knelt down with her and told her I needed her help. That there were a great many people waiting for the bread, and it would be a very good idea if she could help me put the bread in people's hands after I broke it. She could help me make sure everyone received a piece.

After a moment of thought, she agreed to do that, and she distributed bread with me, with an astonishing show of dignity, even a smile, once.

What was more important? The uninterrupted smooth flow of the distribution of Communion, which would have left Renee alone with her tears and her hurt behind the altar, or her participation in this great and holy celebration?

Children acting like adults in church is not only not important, it's not even desirable, not to mention that it's hardly likely.

Children in worship seem to unlock the Holy Spirit in ways that are unexpected, unpredictable, altogether surprising and indescribably enriching.

Once we start down that road, the Spirit will inevitably quicken our hearts. Priorities become clear. Worship becomes for the people, and of the people, and by the people. Worship is claimed by the entire community.

Every encounter with a child in worship changes the face of the worshiping community. This is a good thing, not something to be feared.

For Reflection:

- Take a few minutes to gather your thoughts about the structure, content, and prayers associated with Holy Communion.
- What do they mean to you?

I want to make a distinction here between structure and form. I am considering structure as the framework of worship. In the Episcopal Church, for example, the structure is the skeleton for "An Order for Eucharist." Structures serve to help define our relationship to God and to each other...to everything sacred.

Structures serve to protect the heart, the living pulse of our mystical experience of God. It's the structure that allows life to break through in new form. It is not necessary or even desirable that we abandon the structures that may frame our Sunday worship.

Picture form as an acorn; it has to break in order that new life come forth. It's the form of our worship that deserves our scrutiny. The goal is to hold the forms loosely, to adapt and reconfigure them in the light of the spiritual and liturgical character of the community.

I cannot say enough about the freedom of the Spirit as she is loosed from the bonds and the weight of the forms of our tradition.

Four Table Actions

The scriptural accounts of the Last Supper, are several, and varied; the source material is varied as well. Much, but not all, of what we know as the Institution Narrative, comes from the early writings of Paul, adapted in different ways and for different purposes by the gospel writers.

Moreover, our eucharistic prayers, designed to evoke the imagery and the action from the last meal Jesus is reported to have shared with his friends, often attempt to offer a rationale for Jesus' death in terms of their doctrinal content. This is true both within and across denominational boundaries.

How do we make the decisions about the language and theological content of our eucharistic prayers when our worshiping community includes our children?

Not forgetting that what we know as Sunday worship also serves as a powerful teaching curriculum, what do we need to be teaching our children and each other, in support of our experience of Holy Communion?

Opt for simplicity. Gregory Dix wrote, "At the heart of it all is the eucharistic action, a thing of absolute simplicity—the taking, blessing, breaking and giving of bread and the taking, blessing, and giving of a cup of wine, as these were first done by a young Jew before and after supper with His friends on the night before He died. He had told His friends to do this henceforward with the new meaning for the anamnesis of Him, and they have done it ever since."

For those of you who are eucharistic people, whose heart of worship is Holy Communion, consider carefully the eucharistic prayers you use most often. Break them down into their component parts.

The ones we use most frequently carry four threads: Jesus gives thanks for the bread and the wine; he breaks the bread and identifies it with his body and he identifies the wine with his blood; he asks his disciples to continue this action in remembrance of him; he sends the Holy Spirit into our midst.

"At the heart of it all is the eucharistic action, a thing of absolute simplicity—the taking, blessing, breaking and giving of bread and the taking, blessing, and giving of a cup of wine, as these were first done by a young Jew before and after supper with His friends on the night before He died. He had told His friends to do this henceforward with the new meaning for the anamnesis of Him, and they have done it ever since." Dom Gregory Dix, *The Shape of the Liturgy*.

This, then, becomes the structure for our weekly eucharistic prayer: thanksgiving; the bread broken and the wine poured out; remembrance; the invocation of the Holy Spirit.

Once we disrobe the prayer, peeling it back to its foundational elements, it is no great leap to reconstruct it in such a way that it is accessible to all the members of our congregations, adults and children alike.

Once the structure is in place, seasonal variations are simple. Here are two examples.

Second Sunday of Easter: Thomas the Doubter

The grace of our Lord Jesus Christ be with you all.
And also with you.

Lift up your hearts.
We lift them up to the Lord.

Let us give thanks to the Lord our God.
It is right to give God thanks and praise.

It is right, Holy One, to give you thanks and praise, as we continue our Easter celebration remembering Thomas, the disciple who asked only to see and to touch the wounds in Jesus' hands and side. Confessing our unbelief, it is right to praise you as we sing:

The Sanctus

(The Sanctus is used in many liturgical services to introduce the prayer of Holy Communion. In the Episcopal tradition, the priest and the congregation say or sing this together.)

Holy, Holy, Holy Lord. God of power and might.
Heaven and earth are full of your glory.
Hosannah in the highest.
Blessed is he who comes in the name of the Lord.
Hosannah in the highest.

(Then we continue the prayer of consecration.)

On the night before he died, Jesus gathered his friends together at a table to share a meal. And as they began to eat, he lifted up the bread and the wine to God and gave thanks. It is God who makes the seed for the wheat and the seed for the grape. It is right to thank you.

After he gave thanks, Jesus broke the bread and he broke it again and again. He broke it to remind us that this bread, given by God and broken for us, is bread to feed the whole world. No one need go hungry if she eats this bread. No child, no adult, no elder. This bread, broken, is bread for the children of the world.

And he broke this bread to remind us that God comes to us in those places where we are broken inside. Where we are lonely, frightened, sick, and in sorrow.

As he gave the bread to his disciples he said, "Take, eat: This is my Body which is given for you. Do this for the remembrance of me."

He gave them the cup of wine and said, "Drink this, all of you. This is my Blood of the new Covenant, shed for you and shed for all. Whenever you drink it, do this for the remembrance of me."

That night at the table, Jesus asked one thing of the disciples. He asked them to remember him. Remember him. And so we do remember. We remember today his rising from the grave, the people disbelieving for fear and joy. We remember our own unbelief.

Finally, Jesus made his disciples a promise which he makes to us this day. "I will never leave you alone. I will send God's Holy Spirit to fill your hearts and your minds and your hands."

We ask now that the Holy Spirit of God fill this bread, this cup, and our own hearts as we say together the words that Jesus taught us.

All say **The Lord's Prayer.**

Earth Day

The grace of our Lord Jesus Christ be with you all.
And also with you.

Lift up your hearts.
We lift them up to the Lord.

Let us give thanks to the Lord our God.
It is right to give God thanks and praise.

It is right, Holy One, to give you thanks and praise, as we embrace the gift of your planet, the earth, solid beneath our feet, and her creatures including ourselves, the winged creatures of the air, thanks and praise for the oceans and the lakes and the creatures of the waters.

All say or sing the **Sanctus.**

On the night before he died, Jesus gathered his friends together at a table to share a meal. And as they began to eat, he lifted up the bread and the wine to God and gave thanks. It is God who makes the seed for the wheat and the seed for the grape. It is right to thank you.

After he gave thanks, Jesus broke the bread and he broke it again and again. He broke it to remind us of the body broken, the earth plundered, her creatures destroyed, her air and her waters polluted, the land stripped of its growth.

And he broke this bread to remind us that God comes to us in those places where we are broken inside. Where we are lonely, frightened, sick and in sorrow.

As he gave the bread to his disciples he said, "Take, eat: This is my Body which is given for you. Do this for the remembrance of me."

He gave them the cup of wine and said, "Drink this, all of you. This is my Blood of the new Covenant, shed for you and shed for all. Whenever you drink it, do this for the remembrance of me."

That night at the table, Jesus asked one thing of the disciples. He asked them to remember him. Remember him. And so we do remember. We remember today Jesus at one with the earth and the waters, his calming the seas, his lowly birth in the company of oxen and sheep and goats.

Finally, Jesus made his disciples a promise which he makes to us this day. "I will never leave you alone. I will send God's Holy Spirit to fill your hearts and your minds and your hands."

We ask now that the Holy Spirit of God fill this bread, this cup, and our own hearts as we say together the words that Jesus taught us.

All say **The Lord's Prayer.**

Family Participation

From time to time I will ask a family to do some homework. I will ask them to take a piece of the eucharistic prayer home with them. The thanksgiving piece is perhaps the least threatening. I ask them to talk among themselves as a family, at dinner, in the car after school, at bedtime.

I ask them, "What are you thankful for? What do you count as your blessings, your God-given gifts? Would you share those with us next Sunday, as a family?"

On the designated Sunday, that family will stand at the appropriate time in the eucharistic prayer and share their conversation over the week. It is powerful witness.

One Sunday a father and his two daughters took on the charge of speaking to the broken body. This was a man, in the throes of divorce, who could claim on that day, for himself and his family, 131 days of sobriety. Jesus broke the bread to remind us that God comes to you in your broken places, where you are hurt and frightened and alone.

This was the beginning of a powerful partnership between church and family, where one supports the other.

One Sunday a father and his two daughters agreed to speak about brokenness. This is a man, in the throes of divorce, who could claim on that day, for himself and his family, 131 days of sobriety.

New Opportunities

The first step to including children in worship is very simple. We have to commit to gather the entire community for worship. After that, it will become very clear very quickly what is required of us as liturgical leaders. What adults suffer in liturgy with nothing more than an occasional yawn or lapse of attention, children will not.

The children themselves are our instructors.

Once Sunday worship comes to include the whole community, the changes that we only dare dream about on paper and in theory begin to work themselves.

Thanksgiving Day Service

At Holy Family, we could never anticipate our Thanksgiving Day congregation, neither in terms of numbers, nor age. Some years we've seen only familiar faces. Others, not a single familiar face. Some years perhaps twenty of the forty or so gathered are children. Another year, not even a handful under the age of twelve.

We prepare as best we can for most anything. Stuffed animals at the entrance. Paper and crayons for drawing. Index cards and pens for prayers. Confession stones. Simple, familiar music.

Last Thanksgiving Day morning I arrived at nine o'clock for a ten o'clock service of Holy Communion. Due to a family crisis the night before, I had prepared nothing. No printed Orders of Service. Not even a sermon.

I sat in the kitchen over a cup of coffee and the lessons assigned for the day, in the Episcopal Lectionary: Deuteronomy 8:1–3, 6–20; James 1:17–18, 21–27; Matthew 6:25–33.

The Deuteronomy lesson makes the connection between the following of the Law and the gift of the Promised Land. "You must observe everything that I command you this day, so that you may live and increase and occupy the land which the Lord has promised."

The letter from James speaks of being born into the truth and calls us to godly action.

And from the Gospel of Matthew, familiar and comforting language about the lilies of the field. "Put away anxious thoughts. Consider how the lilies grow in the fields. They do not work. They do not spin. And yet, I tell you, even Solomon in all his splendor was not clothed like one of these."

I read over these lessons in sequence: Hebrew Scripture, epistle, gospel. Most of us are accustomed to an order of worship, one which is generally linear: we move from the Liturgy of the Word to the Liturgy of the Table. So, to speak about reading in sequence is nothing out of the ordinary.

But as I was reading the lessons, the actions from the Liturgy of the Table kept intruding. First a lesson, then an action from the table. Another lesson, another action from the table. The entire service reranged itself like this:

Liturgy of the Word

The law and the commandments are the backbones of our lives. God says, obey the Law that I give you in order that you may live and bear fruit. The Torah is the gift of life. (De)

We are born into the truth. The truth breaks us. Unless we are broken we do not know the truth. (Ja)

We are called to godly action. Be sure that you act on the message and not merely listen. (Ja)

We are adorned by God's grace. Consider the lilies of the field, they neither toil nor spin. (Mt)

Liturgy of the Table

All our gifts come from God. What we eat, what we drink. It is right to give God thanks and praise.

Jesus breaks bread for the world. He reminds us that God reaches into our broken places.

We remember Jesus, the works that he accomplished. His teaching and preaching, his healing the sick and his casting out of demons.

Jesus promises us the gift of the Holy Spirit. May it fill this bread, this cup. May it fill our hearts.

For Reflection:

Select the Lectionary readings for a Sunday of your choice.
Lay out the Liturgy of the Word and the Liturgy of the Table as illustrated in this text.
What points of correspondence do you discover?
What might it be like to develop and experience service of worship "in the round"?

This excited me. The possibility of a service of Holy Communion developed, not in linear or sequential fashion, but in the round, had not ever occurred to me.

We tried it.

We set up circular seating with the table within the circle at its perimeter.

We gathered the congregants with the Prayers of the People.

We read a lesson, reflected, and commented upon it. We followed the reading with the corresponding piece of the table liturgy.

We read the first part of the second lesson, reflected, and made comment. We broke the bread.

We read the second part of the second lesson, and remembered the works of Jesus.

We stood for the gospel, invoked the Holy Spirit, and distributed the gifts of bread and wine, each of us communicating the next.

It was a powerful morning. The liturgy of Holy Communion came alive in a way that defied analysis. The Spirit had graced us, and people departed that morning having been deeply touched.

I've done a great deal of thinking since that morning. How did that happen? I had not set out to alter in any way our traditional Thanksgiving Day liturgy.

I can only attribute it to a spiritual evolution which takes place when an entire community including its children agree to worship together. The forms yield when they have to for the sake of the spiritual deepening of a congregation.

Christmas Eve

As we began preparations for Christmas, a parent of a five-year-old and a two-year-old left a Christmas story entitled "A Small Miracle" (Peter Collington, Alfred A. Knopf, 1997) on my desk.

With paintings only, no words, it shows the story of an old woman who lives alone in her shack. One morning she rises from her bed, stretches, and goes to her cupboard for something to eat. There is nothing, not in her cupboards, not on the shelves, not on her stove. There is no money in her money box.

She takes her accordion, treks across fields covered with snow, to the center of town, where she plays in the hopes of earning a dollar or two. Shoppers pass by, hurrying. No one drops a coin in her box. The woman, defeated, sells her accordion to the pawnbroker and receives a few dollars in exchange. But, as she leaves, she is accosted by a thief on a motorcycle, who steals her money. She gives chase, and follows his tire tracks to the church.

Just as she reaches the church door, the thief bursts through it, the alms box tight in his hand. This time the old woman fights him, and succeeds in reclaiming the money for the church. She enters the door, only to find that the entire crèche scene lies scattered over the floor.

After restoring order in the crèche and the church, the old woman starts out for home, across the same fields she had navigated earlier. But she's had nothing to eat, and she collapses in the snow, cold, hungry, exhausted, and alone.

But...the crèche figures come to life. They race across the fields, carry the woman to her shack, put her in her bed. The shepherds cut wood for a fire. Mary sings her a song. The Magi make the journey back to the pawnshop, where they redeem her accordion with their gold and frankincense and myrrh, buy food for her dinner, and return to her shack.

They cut her a tree, cook her a magnificent dinner, and then disappear, back to the church.

The old woman wakes up, looks around, rubbing her eyes in disbelief, then sits at her table to eat her dinner, and after her meal, picks up her beloved accordion and plays.

I read this beautiful story with no words from cover to cover, and knew immediately that the children of our congregation could act it out in tableaux. And then, for the second time, the liturgy of Holy Communion began to rearrange itself.

The first section of the story, in which the old woman, hungry and penniless, is forced to pawn her accordion, corresponded to the broken body. Jesus says, "This is my body, broken for you."

And so on this Christmas Eve, we wove together the first part of the story with the breaking action of the table.

What you would see if you were in the congregation would be a drama, with the focus, first on the story, then, on the table.

Then back to the story, the next piece of which, as the woman is mugged and beaten and is left to die in the snow, corresponds to Jesus' trial and sentence and death on the cross. We move to the table liturgy. Jesus says, "Whenever you do this, do it in remembrance of me."

The crèche figures come to life and revive the old woman, carrying her into her shack, fixing her meal, redeeming her accordion. Jesus says, "I will not leave you comfortless. I will send the Spirit upon you." The action shifts to the invocation of the Holy Spirit at the table liturgy.

The only departure from the story itself was that in the final scene, the old woman celebrated her meal, not at a small table in her own shack by herself. She shared that meal with the rest of us at one table, in the center of the sanctuary.

And of course, it being Christmas Eve, we concluded our service with hymns and carols of thanksgiving and praise for the gift of new life.

Spilling Over

The Holy Spirit has not been content to contain herself to worship with children. Take, for example, the two liturgies outlined above. The experience on both occasions was one of pure grace, and neither was designed solely around children.

The celebrations we are coming to share are no longer about children only. They are about community, and everything that happens or begins to happen within our family service spills over and has application in other areas of our congregational life.

Another Application

Consider "liturgy in the round," in which the Liturgy of the Word and personal reflection and the Liturgy of the Table are woven on circular needles.

This became an option for funerals.

Think about what we do in our Burial Rites.

We give thanks for the life we now mourn. We express our own brokenness and the brokenness of the grieving community. We remember the life we celebrate. We invoke the Holy Spirit, asking her into the hearts of those who grieve.

Each of those eucharistic aspects is reflected in the Word—the readings chosen to honor this life, the eulogy, the prayers.

The correspondence is exact.

Opt for the Children

To make the decision to include children as full members of the worshiping community changes how we do things. None of us expects that this can be accomplished without anxiety, without stress, without resistance, without fear.

Congregations are more likely to embrace the baptismal theology of the full inclusion of children and youth in worship, than they are to welcome the practical implications of such commitments.

I don't know of and have not yet worked with any congregation in which resistance to these kinds of changes has not been of primary significance (see Chapter 9). Know you are not alone, and not

Take one step, just one step. You will find that the community's transformation, resulting from that one step, becomes the foundation of faith and courage for the next step. That's a promise.

working in a vacuum. Asking people to reflect upon their patterns and habits of worship, and then to change those patterns which do not serve the entire community, is provocative business.

But not only do I believe we must do it, I know with certainty the urgency that drives the challenge.

Before the first step, where most of us find ourselves—a heart that's willing and a mind that sees the need, but the courage of the cowardly lion—the task seems overwhelming, and of course it is.

But it doesn't happen all at once. It's an evolutionary process.

Take one step. Just one step. You will find that the community's transformation resulting from that one step, becomes the foundation of faith and courage for the next step.

That's a promise.

Paint the Stories

Faith is an "Acoustical Affair"

I have heard it said that faith is an "acoustical affair," meaning that you catch it by listening to the Word. This is not the only way. We catch the faith through art as well, through drawing, painting, dance, and music.

Art is a powerful vehicle for the expression of faith.

I rarely consider the illustrations contained in Sunday school curricula as art, and the resistance I experience often has less to do with theological content than it does with what passes for art. I confess a bias against coloring book pictures of Jesus and little wooly sheep with smiles across their faces. I do not believe that the miracles of God can be contained within borders and assigned certain colors. Nor do I believe that church-related art ought to be relegated to the family refrigerator for a week or so and then tossed with the trash.

Liturgical art needs to be seen. Hung. Used. Worn. Sung. Acted.

The ways in which glitter, yarn, papier mâché, musical notes, spices, gestures, ink, paint, and typeface can be attached to paper, cloth, pianos, and even bodies, for liturgical uses, are infinite.

I return again to that lone voice from the heart of our discussions about children and worship, "If we are still going to separate the children from the rest of the congregation, then the children should be in the church and the adults in the classrooms."

In this chapter I include examples of the art produced on a weekly basis by the children of Holy Family Church. The children have come to expect the opportunity to express their deepening faith and spiritual journeys in art and drama and poetry and music. They have no self-consciousness about this. Children do it naturally.

Take advantage of the artistic gifts of your children. Let them show the rest of us the integral part that art plays in the worship life of a congregation.

117

Sunday School or No Sunday School?

The commitment of the Holy Family congregation was to inclusive worship. Children and youth became an integral part of worship, participating in the music, the Liturgy of the Word, the prayers, confession, peace, and Prayer of Consecration.

Still, the adults expressed their need and desire for adult time. As our community negotiated its decisions, we agreed upon this pattern.

The first piece of it was a concept we came to understand as self-selection. No one was required to stay in the service. Child care was always provided. For toddlers, it fell to the parents to make the decision as to their inclusion. Children above the age of three generally made their own choices.

Nor was anyone required to leave.

Secondly, we designed the service with the intention of full inclusion through communion. The storytelling, prayers, and the confession and eucharistic prayers were developed as described in earlier chapters.

Following the distribution of communion, the children and youth generally exercised their option to leave, while the adults exercised theirs to stay for several minutes of quiet prayer and a sermon, the same sermon preached at the earlier, more traditional service.

It was during this block of twenty to thirty minutes (and longer, if there were projects to finish) that the children would do their art.

Art as the Backdrop of Worship

The children should be in the church where there is beauty: rich vestments and altar linens, music, candles, brass, painting, sculpture, and music.

Those words sparked the onset of a liturgical project at Holy Family that has served us well for years. We cut out countless squares of muslin fabric, and asked the members of our congregation, young and old, to draw a godly symbol on a square. We then sewed them together to create a full altar set—frontal, two stoles, a chasuble, a lectern hanging, a veil, and a burse, which we would used every week during the season after Pentecost.

We painted square after square, piling them up for our resident seamstress.

Peace symbols. Rainbows and flowers. A Star of David stands out as though some young prophet knew that within a few years we would be exploring space-sharing possibilities with the Coastside Jewish Community.

One square, bottom center, reads "All God's Creatures are Welcome Here."

And on the altar itself, representative of those creatures and reminiscent of Isaiah's prophecy, "the lion and the lamb shall lie down together," live our own well-worn, much-loved ancient versions.

All God's Creatures are Welcome Here

The lion and the lamb shall lie down together

Creating seasonal frontals became for us an intergenerational project. With just a little forethought, art tasks can be assigned from the youngest to the oldest.

We use this activity to teach not only the story itself. We add first century flavor as well, as evidenced by the Christmas frontal, below.

"The day came for the child to be delivered"

We colored with first-century spices, garlic and cardamon.

We researched weather patterns and constellations.

And then we divided up the tasks, beginning with the toddlers who made stars from aluminum foil.

Our donkeys had gold glitter eyes, and our cradle had straw from the pony farm next door. Our sheep were clothed in yarn, and their hooves sparkled with silver.

A richly textured piece.

One of our teens opted for a window to the great outdoors.

Although this particular frontal was put together on butcher block paper, it has proved indestructible, and has served Holy Family well for many Christmas seasons.

Others we made on the day of a particular story, for example, Jesus walking on the water. We then put the frontal away until the next time we read the story.

Watching the children of Holy Family remember their work—"I did Jesus' feet"—is an exquisite pleasure. The children catch a glimpse of the frontal, and the story is spilling off their tongues.

Art connects in powerful and surprising ways. We know this as adults. Let us not forget how it is with children.

For Reflection:

Where does the "Word, Truth, Beauty, and love of God" happen in worship?

Making Connections

I cannot help but be reminded here of the seven-year-old boy, whom I mentioned in Chapter 4. When his grandfather brought him to the church for the first time. He joined us at the altar for the eucharistic liturgy, and when he heard the news of the crucifixion, he said loudly and unabashedly, "You mean he died?"

You mean he died?

It was a question not unlike the question that Peter raised when Jesus told him of his approaching death.

The child's older brother, who was already wise in the ways of the holy, elbowed him in the ribs and said, "Yes he died. That's the way it is with God."

That is as good a description of the task we set for ourselves as worship communities as any I can think of. We remember how it is with God.

Our task is to develop an environment so filled with images and art and symbols of God, to recreate with our own hands and our own tongues such a portrait of God's redemptive work, to show by the way we are with one another the irresistible reconciling love of God, that we never never forget how it is with God.

With that in mind, every moment carries the seed of a teaching moment, especially the ones, like the one mentioned above, that are unplanned.

The job of the seven-year-olds of the world is to wreak havoc with the things we take for granted.

Jesus died. When was the last time that surprised you?

The question that congregations need to ask on a weekly basis is this: How do we develop worship in such a way that moments like these are not only possible and tolerated, but anticipated and welcomed?

Once the question is asked, the promise is one of abundance. A process begins. A piece falls into place. Another piece is added onto that one. Then another and another. The process becomes a way of life.

King of Kings

One day, for no particular reason, a doll appeared. Someone had donated it, someone thinking ahead to the next barn sale, perhaps. It was a big doll, perhaps two feet tall, made of cloth. It was unclothed.

Someone rescued him from the barn and brought him into the church.

In preparation for the Feast of the Epiphany, the children and youth of Holy Family decided to dress the doll in an outfit befitting a Middle Eastern king.

They liked him. They decided to include him in the procession on the first Sunday of Epiphany, and every Sunday following.

By the time a week or two had passed, every adult and teen and child in our congregation—member or friend or first-time visitor—knew we were in the season of Epiphany.

We made a new outfit for Lent and another for Easter.

Our king keeps track of the liturgical seasons.

Our King keeps track of the liturgical seasons

The Bathroom Series

Not far along into the season of Lent one year, I was musing about the walls of our handicapped access bathroom. It's a large, fairly elegant bathroom, with shiny lava tiles on the floor, and quite a bit of empty wall space. A plan began to emerge.

Our children would do a panel-by-panel representation of the life of Jesus to form an upper border along the walls. We would begin with Gabriel's announcement to Mary, her pregnancy, and the subsequent birth of the child. We would move through Epiphany, Lent, Holy Week, Good Friday, Easter, and Pentecost.

Our new doll, appropriately clothed for each season, would sit on a three-legged stool, and the stool would shift with the seasons, at one time, under the eastern star and the camels, another time under the cross, another time, under the empty tomb.

Anyone going into that bathroom would know in an instant the current liturgical season.

And, to the extent possible, we would ask each child to create her own life story, corresponding at appropriate points, to the life story of Jesus. Their births, their visitors, their Baptisms, their lost and lonely places, the stories of children engaged with the story of Jesus.

We call this our "Bathroom Series," first, because that's where we began it, but second, and more important, because we strive to connect to God in the very ordinary occasions of our lives.

So many times we hear people say, "We don't know what do to with the children." Or, "I'm not creative enough to work with children." Or, "I'm not an artist." Or, "We don't know how to begin it."

To all those voices saying, "I can't," we say, "Just start." And before you even know what has happened to you, you will look at a story and know the drama, look at a wall and know what it needs. The work spills over, even into the bathroom.

Soon we had more panels than wall space, which allowed us to choose our historical or liturgical emphasis at any given moment. It allowed us to add panels depicting never-before-thought-of occasions of Jesus' life. It serves our community as a powerful teaching tool.

Making Connections

The child whose idea it was to have Mary's belly protrude with her pregnancy, confided one day that the baby was a boy. "You can tell because she's carrying it low."

Some time after we'd finished that panel and it was hanging in place, a four-year-old girl brought me a copy of a sonogram. "This is me," she said. "But nobody would know. It could go up there with Mary."

We put a frame around it and hung the sonogram on Mary's wall.

To all those voices saying, "I can't," we say, "Just start." And before you even know what has happened to you, you will look at a story and know the drama, look at a wall and know what it needs. The work spills over, even into the bathroom.

Making Connections

All God's Creatures are Welcome

"Look," one of the young artists remarks. "That donkey is smiling."

"All the animals are smiling," another child points out.

"They're smiling because they're happy. They're smiling because they're a part of things.

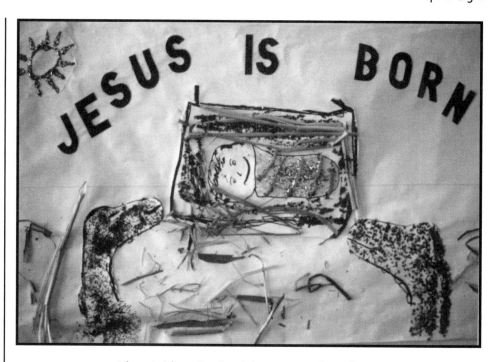

The stable animals with grins on their faces

Bearing Gifts

We talk about what we would bring to Jesus. "I'd bring him a jacket." "I'd bring him a doll." "A doll? He's a boy!" "So? I'd bring him a boy doll."

"I'd bring him a fire engine."
"I'd bring him my lunch."
"I'd bring him my heart. "

Kings come, bearing gifts

The Ordinariness of Things

We fill in other parts of the story. Jesus learns to spell; he learns to read. Jesus helps Mary. The children all laugh when they think about Jesus having to do chores. Jesus gets lost. We talk about moments in our lives that we've been lost.

Jesus is Baptized

"John the Baptist did the baptizing. He was Jesus' cousin."

"John didn't want to do it. He said Jesus should be the one baptizing him."

"Yeah, but John the Baptist was already baptized. So, how could Jesus baptize him again?"

I am reminded of my first and my second Baptisms. Good questions.

Jesus is Baptized

On to Jerusalem

"That's supposed to be a scowl, not a smile. You can tell by his eyebrows."

"Those donkeys didn't ask for the job."

"That's for sure."

The children themselves express anger as they're doing this panel. You can see it on their faces. You can see it in the way they cut with the scissors, the way they smear the glue on the paper.

Jesus turns his face to Jerusalem

Jesus Dies on the Cross

"Let's make the other two crosses on this one."
"Why?"
"Because then he won't be so lonely."
"Okay."

It's a wonderful experience to see the children working as a group, making decisions together, the theological decisions as well as the artistic ones. Pay attention to the rich conversations of the children as they do this work.

Jesus is Crucified, and the Two Thieves With Him

"I like the way the story ends."

"Yeah, me too."

I ask them if they think the story has really ended, and as we talk about it, we agree that it hasn't.

He is Risen!

Mask Making: Spillover Art

As a congregation's children begin to develop increasingly sophisticated artwork, the comments from the adults begin to change. "I can't do something like that" changes to "Hmmm, that looks like fun."

"I'm not an artist" changes to "I wonder if I could try something like that."

"Art is just for the children" becomes, "You know, I think I could do with a little right brain development myself." We call that "spillover art."

One summer we offered a Wednesday evening intergenerational community art session which we entitled, "Summer Fun."

We gathered each week for two hours. Some of us brought beads, others knitting or crochet. We sketched, painted, and sculpted with clay.

Several of us had expressed a desire to make masks, and with that in mind, we decided to undertake a project for the church.

We crafted wire mesh armatures and went to work with newspaper, flour, and water.

We used the masks we made on several occasions during the course of the year: Pentecost and Trinity Sunday, Earth Day, All Saints, and other occasions we deemed appropriate.

Worshipers of all ages are transported into deep spiritual pockets through the use of masks. We have others besides our Trinity. We have evil faces and child faces and old faces and clear plastic faces which we use in our drama throughout the year.

The following are examples.

Ancient of Days

The Ancient One presides at Holy Communion. With a wisdom that needs no words, the gestures of the Ancient One are powerful and expansive.

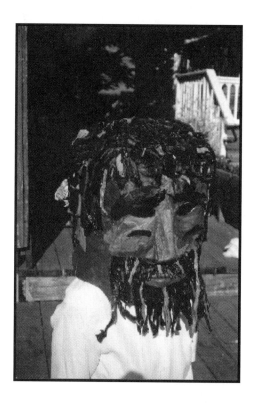

The Ancient One: the Creator God

Lion of Judah

The Revelation of John (5:5) makes reference to the Lion of Judah: "See, the Lion of the tribe of Judah, the Root of David, has conquered, so that he can open the scroll and its seven seals."

Our Lion of Judah associates himself with the Word, holding the Gospel book while someone reads from behind him.

The Lion of Judah

...and a dove descended

This gentle winged creature has made her way from the West Coast to Las Vegas to Chicago to Philadelphia, where she dances her way through the prayers and table feasts of countless congregations.

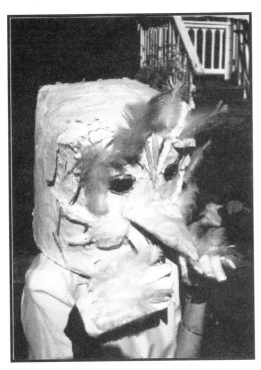

Spirit Bird

First Fruits

When I was a child, the hero in one of my favorite stories was named Bartholomew. He was a young child, probably seven or eight, and he stood along the side of the road waiting for the queen to pass by in her carriage. As she drew closer, Bartholomew took off his hat, as was the custom, but another appeared in its place. He removed that one as well, and yet another appeared. And another and another.

Art is like that. The more we do, the more we have to do. Using art and music and drama as the building blocks for faith development has had surprising and transformational moments, and has led to an inexhaustible energy and commitment to do more.

The generosity of the children was a surprise as well. Children have donated their work not only for the congregation of Holy Family, but also for the wider community that the parish serves.

We Reach Out

I am struck over and again by the generosity of children, particularly as it has to do with making a gift of their art, a gift not only to the church, but to the world.

It's as though the very creating of beauty inspires the giving away of it. Art, I believe, quickens the heart and moves it in the direction of generosity. The mere act of creating seems to inspire one to keep on giving it to the world.

When one of the young adults of our congregation went to work in Alaska for a month during the summer, the children of Holy Family sent hand-drawn and constructed cards of greeting to the children of Fort Yukon and Venetie.

When a friend of our congregation came to talk to the children about his forthcoming visit to Haiti and one of the Haitian orphanages where he'd be staying, they made a card for every child, this time attaching bubble gum, Polaroid photos of themselves, and chocolate Kisses.

God is generous like that, I think, and the children know this.

Given the opportunity, it is children who teach adults about creative generosity. Theirs is a voice integral to the health of a community, and we do ourselves grave disservice to send those voices down some dusty stairs into church basement after church basement so the adults can have their worship time in the church.

Children do not need the artistic constraints of Sunday school curricula. I tend to think it's the "adult-within-us-who-cannot-draw" who needs that kind of standardized form.

Imagine the richness and the depth of the story of Jesus when depicted by a child in the discovery phase of faith. Color, texture, plot, song, drama, dance. All come alive! We adults do not have to do the work for our children. All we have to do is step back. Get out of the way.

Think in terms of seasons of the church year. What teaching projects might you develop through the many facets of artistic composition that would serve to break open the Good News of Christ?

Imagine it like looking through the several facets of a prism; the heart of the gospel is inside. Think about plumbing its depths in one way and then another and another.

For Reflection:

Think in terms of seasons of the church year. What teaching projects might you develop through the many facets of artistic composition that would serve to break open the Good News of Christ?

Extended Projects

Extended projects are valuable for several reasons. First, they offer children the opportunity to engage in spiritual conversation at ever deepening levels. Second, when the children have still more to do on the projects, they keep coming back.

Several years ago we asked the children of Holy Family to embark with us on the journey of Lent. We told the story of the Baptism of Jesus and his subsequent days and nights in the desert.

"What might we need for such a journey?" we asked them.

Two responses came back almost immediately.

"A suitcase!"

"Feet!"

We embarked on our Lenten project.

First Sunday of Lent

Following communion, the children came from the church to the art rooms. There they each cut (or had someone cut for them) two panels from bright red poster board, in the shape of hearts. They punched holes along the sides, and stitched them together with yarn, all but the tops. They stapled a braid of yarn to the panels, for a handle. Voila! A suitcase.

Second Sunday of Lent

The children made feet out of yellow poster board. Some of the children painted the poster board toes with glitter. These feet were going to do a lot of journeying. They wanted them to be strong. They wanted them to look good. They didn't want to scare people away with their feet!

Third Sunday of Lent

What else might be needed for the journey?

"Hands. The hands of God in the world!"

The children made hands, again of poster board, for strength and durability. Some were small, others huge. Some had old, tired veins. Some were smooth. Many had painted fingernails. And all the while the children were sharing stories of trips they had taken. Good times, hard times. Some were for pleasure. Others to visit a sick or dying relative.

Fourth Sunday of Lent

Next, they made eyes and ears and mouths, glued them to one side of the suitcase. They decorated them with dried herbs and spices, spoke about the kinds of food that were eaten in the time of Jesus. They shared their conviction regarding the importance of the senses of taste, vision, hearing, touch, and smell.

When you decide to do an extended project like this one, it is a good idea to make extra sets of materials for the children who are absent one week and present the next. It's a good idea to have materials available for any visitors.

Fifth Sunday of Lent

Finally, the children decided to make maps for the other side of the suitcase. Where did they want to go during their lives? These were wonderful maps—part geography, part dream and hope and vision.

By the end of Lent, they were packed and ready. They put their suitcases aside until Easter.

Easter Sunday

The children spoke of the Resurrection of Jesus in terms of the symbol of a butterfly. They removed the feet from their suitcases. Each foot became the body of a butterfly, and because each child had two feet, we had plenty for Easter visitors. They decorated the body of each butterfly, cut out wings of new poster board and decorated them. The several adults in the room stapled wings and elastic bands to the body parts, so that each child could wear a Resurrection butterfly as an arm band.

They accomplished these things in the art rooms during the twenty minutes that followed communion. As the post Communion hymn began, they danced back into the church, seventy children or more, the symbol of the Risen Christ on their shoulders.

We hadn't planned the butterflies. We hadn't planned beyond the suitcase. But the Spirit had claimed us, and the transformational piece from Lent to Easter was accomplished.

Two weeks later, the bombing of the Oklahoma City federal building screamed over the news. Without much discussion at all, the children of Holy Family packed up almost eighty suitcases and butterflies and sent them to the Episcopal Diocese of Oklahoma, asking that their gifts be distributed among the children of the diocese.

Make A Book

One Sunday after church, two ten-year-old girls asked me for an appointment.

"How about next Saturday?" I suggested.

That was fine.

When they came into my office, they told me about their idea.

"We want to write a book." one said.

"We want to draw a book," the other said.

"We want to write and draw a book."

"Then we want to sell it and give the money to some special places."

The special organizations included a coastal organization which undertakes the cleaning of oil from spills from the ocean birds and mammals. Another distributes vouchers to pay for the vaccinations of the dogs and the cats of the people who live on the streets.

We talked for a long time that morning. They were thinking about art and poetry and songs and prayers. The cover of *The Art of Children* was painted by an eight-year-old child.

"All the kids can do stuff," they assured me.

We talked and plotted and planned. We took a field trip to the tide pools near the church. Bit by bit, the poetry and the paintings and the prayers dribbled in.

And a book was made.

Erin, a ten-year-old, has taken responsibility for much of the poetry in the book. She has a powerful voice, and a sensitive one. With her permission, I include several of her poems.

Miracle in Spring

I see a meadow in spring.
It seems that elves must have come
to paint this rolling meadow
with the colors of the sun
with the bright blue of the sky
and with iridescent purple.
Now it's sprinkling lightly
But it's still sunny and warm.
A double rainbow spreads across the sky.

A small doe and fawn swiftly glide
across the field.
A blue jay perches upon a tree
that's rich in milk-white blossoms
And I wouldn't be surprised if a miracle
happened today.

Night

Darkness comes,
bearing stars,
like diamonds in the sky.
Crescent moon,
giving just enough light
to see all the creatures
who come alive only at night.

War

It has rained and now it's sunny.
There should be a rainbow in the sky.
There should be people laughing.
But instead the people cry,
as a bomb drops from up high.

The Homeless Woman

She's shivering.
Sleet is pouring.
I'm quivering.
I want to do something for her.
She's homeless.
I reach into my pocket
No money at all.
All I have is a credit card and a locket.
Snow starts to fall.
I run into the store.
I charge a rain jacket and a large fleece throw.
I wish I could do more.
It makes me feel better than she could ever know
When I was kind to that woman on the street.

Jungle

A gunshot, a cry,
"Yippee" is the hunter's reply
to the dying tiger's roar.
To him there's no pain,
to him it is plain,
there are plenty of tigers in this jungle.
The tiger shudders as if she's cold
and ignores the pain in her breast,
to lick her cubs one last time,
before eternal rest.

I Am...

I am River,
power-mad river,
strong and mighty
and bold

I am Creek,
like melted diamonds
soft as silk

Hidden Tears

Quietly crying
Softly bending
Constantly trying
to hide its tears inside its leaves.
That's why it bends and droops
And no one knows why the weeping willow weeps.

Rain

I am life to the flowers,
the trees,
and the people.
I fill pools to the brim.
I wash all things clean.
I am holy,
though I was never blessed.
I am Rain.

Night

I envelop all,
I bring the owl, the mouse and the bat,
the stars and the moon are my companions.
I am the Night.

For Reflection:

- The poetry of our children has become the foundation for our exchange of the Good News. During the gospel time we read a poem, and we talk about it.
- How does this poem carry the seed of God's love, we ask?
- How does this poem work to transform our attitudes and our appetites?
- Create for your children a safe place to express themselves, and then honor them for their expression.

I Want to Be

I want to be an astronaut,
said Little Louie.

I want to be a ballerina, said
Joey.

What silly things to be, cries
Sue.
When you could work in a
zoo!

Quiet little Mina, sitting in
the Corner,

Softy says, I want to be a
Dreamer.

For Reflection:

Ask yourselves these
questions:
- Is your church safe
  for children?
- How do the children
  know that?
- Will you take their
  art and their poetry
  seriously?
- Do you talk to them
  about it?
- How will you incorpo-
  rate it into the litur-
  gical life of your
  community?

Your children can do this. The task of the adults is to create an environment that fosters not only the creativity of children, but also the nurturing of that creativity.

Keep them with you in church. Learn to recognize their ministries. That's not possible if you worship in segregated ways.

Ask yourselves these questions:

Is your church safe for children? How do the children know that? Will you take their art and their poetry seriously? Do you talk to them about it? How will you incorporate it into the liturgical life of your community?

The Angels Have Come

One weekday afternoon in November, near the end of the day and darkness had already dropped, Gwen the music coordinator rushed into my office. Her eyes were shining. "Come," she told me. "I need you to listen."

Gwen teaches piano to young students and the student at her piano that afternoon was a ten-year-old whose name is Missy. Missy is a good student and she has a powerful voice. What neither Gwen nor I knew at that time was that Missy composed music.

Missy had written an Advent song, had put it to music, and now she wanted to know if she could sing it for us.

She did sing it, and with her permission I include it here. Missy sang a solo on the Second Sunday of Advent, and she has been writing music ever since.

You may well have a young composer in your church. Invite your children to create new music. You may be in for wonderful surprises.

Conversations With Fred

Fred was six when I first met him. He seemed at that time to exude the kind of confidence I didn't even dream about as a child. Fred is of Austrian descent and already bilingual, so my first introduction to him sounded like this.

"I'm an arggh-tiste."

A bilingual six-year-old arggh-tiste. Fred wore a beret and carried a paint brush.

When he was seven, he began to take art lessons, working with a Coastside artist named Susan. Susan and Fred began their work together in the nick of time, really, because already there was not much in the world of construction paper and glue that would contain Fred.

One year, as we headed into the season of Lent, Fred turned nine.

Lent, historically, is a season in which we do an extended art project with the children of Holy Family, usually an outreach project. He'd complained of boredom during the previous year's project.

We asked him, "How would you like to paint the Stations of the Cross?"

Fred has a way of focusing his eyes somewhere into the distance. Another galaxy, maybe.

"What are those things...stations?"

We explained about the journey that Jesus himself took.

"How many stations are we talking about?"

"Fourteen," we told him.

"By this year?"

"No. By next year."

Half a beat.

"Okay."

We had no idea what we were asking of a nine-year-old child. Nor did we know until later how the questions might define themselves.

Is it possible for a child to sustain a certain creative energy over the duration of a year? What growth and spiritual deepening might he anticipate? What learning will occur as he connects a life of two thousand years ago with life as he knows it today? What kind of artistic problems will he address and what will his problem solving look like? What might he expect in terms of the expansion of his talent? Will he grow discouraged? Bored?

Fred completed the paintings, and with his permission, I include several of them here. In addition to the artwork itself, I had requested of Fred that we debrief each painting as he accomplished it. Those conversations are included as well.

STATION ONE: JESUS IS CONDEMNED TO DEATH

Fred's decided that it's okay with him if his mother listens in.

We set the first painting against the back of a chair and sat back to look at it.

Fred: It's Pilate and Jesus, together.
Caroline: Where are they, do you think?

Fred:	They're in a room. Nobody else is in the room. But the crowds are in the courtyard down below.
Caroline:	What about the crowds?
Fred:	They're yelling to Pilate to release the other guy...um...
Caroline:	Barabbas?
Fred:	Yeah. They're yelling at Pilate to release Barabbas and kill Jesus.
Caroline:	Is that what Pilate is going to do?
Fred:	Well yeah. That's the story. (Fred didn't want to tolerate my ill-advised questions.)
Caroline:	So, tell me about this painting.
Fred:	Pilate is telling Jesus that he has to die. (We reflected on the painting for a moment.) You know what I like about it?
Caroline:	What?
Fred:	Pilate is telling Jesus he has to die. And the words are hard. (He pointed to the words of condemnation coming from Pilate's mouth.) But they don't touch Jesus, do they. It's like Jesus isn't really affected.
Caroline:	Yes, I see that. Did you mean to do it that way?
Fred:	No. Not really. I noticed it after it was already done. Cool.
Caroline:	Definitely cool. So, if Jesus isn't affected, how do you suppose he's feeling?
Fred:	Jesus is angry. Not about the dying so much. He's angry because he thinks people betrayed him. And he's angry because he wanted to help more, and now he's not going to get the chance.

STATION TWO: JESUS PICKS UP HIS CROSS

We were in Fred's living room. He was seated in one of two overstuffed chairs. I was in the other. I lay this second painting on the floor between us. For a long moment, we just looked at it.

| Fred: | His nose is pretty big. |
| Caroline: | Impressive. How come you painted in black and white? |

Fred has a way of looking slightly past you when you're not being very smart. It's the next best thing to rolling your eyes.

Fred: Think about it, Caroline. It wasn't a very happy time. Jesus wasn't happy. His disciples weren't happy. Mary Magdalene wasn't happy. His other friends weren't happy. His mother wasn't happy. Nobody was very happy. Why would I paint it in color if nobody was happy?

Caroline: What's this? (I was pointing to the backdrop, against which Jesus was walking in profile.)

Fred: That's Calvary.

Caroline: (I nodded) Sun's hot.

Fred: It's hot in the Middle East. Hot in the daytime, anyway.

Caroline: Tell me about these marks on his arm.

Fred: His tunic is ripped. It's torn there.

Caroline: (Looking blank.)

Fred: The wood wasn't smooth then, like it is now. The splinters on the cross tore his shirt.

Caroline: I see. So...how'd you get the hands right. That couldn't have been very easy.

Fred: It wasn't. On the first one I did? I did it in pencil, 'til I got it right. I erased so much I put a hole in the paper. Then I made Nick (his younger brother) hold books in his hands, so I could see how the hands went.

Caroline: How did you feel when you were painting this painting?

Fred: You mean as Fred? Or you mean as Jesus?

Caroline: Both, I guess.

Fred: Well, as Fred, I wasn't sure I could do it. So I was kind of nervous. As Jesus...kinda scared. I guess I'd have been kind of scared.

STATION THREE: JESUS FALLS FOR THE FIRST TIME

I lay the next painting down between us, and we stared at it for a while. Fred shook his head.

Fred:	That was a hard one.
Caroline:	A hard one?
Fred:	Yeah. I tried to do it in profile. I tried a couple times. But I couldn't get it right. So I just did him face down. With the cross smack on top of him.
Caroline:	What do you think?
Fred:	I think it really hurt him. Especially his face, which is right down in the sand. And his ribs, probably. The cross was heavy, don't you think?
Caroline:	Yeah. I do think.
Fred:	Sun's moved a little. It's later in the day.
Caroline:	(I nodded. I was very close to tears.) I see the rips in his shirt.
Fred:	Tunic. (Fred smiled. He didn't want to embarrass me.) Yep. They wouldn't have gone away.

We stared at the painting for a while.

Fred:	Hurts.
Caroline:	Yeah.

STATION FOUR: JESUS MEETS HIS AFFLICTED MOTHER

Before I could even compose the first question, Fred had something to say.

Fred:	They are so happy.
Caroline:	Happy?
Fred:	Jesus is especially happy. He gets to see his mother one more time before he dies. That's important to him.

141

Caroline: What about Mary? Is she happy? Must be hard to watch her son go to his death.

Fred: She's not so happy all the time. But she's happy right at this moment. And she is letting him know how much she loves him.

We were both quiet for a moment, thinking about Mary and Jesus.

Fred: His death will be hard on Jesus, with his mother there. He wants to live so she doesn't have to have that kind of pain. He's worried about her. But look at their eyes. Both of their eyes. They're so focused. They're trying to take a picture of each other with their eyes. So they'll remember. Forever.

I looked at their eyes and realized that Fred was quite right. They were looking at each other as though they would never stop. It was very clear to me that I had a lot to learn.

STATION SIX: A WOMAN WIPES THE FACE OF JESUS

This painting shocked me and I was eager to talk with Fred about it.

Caroline: It's a pretty sophisticated idea, Fred. The image of Jesus' face on the cloth.

Fred: (Nodding.) It's not my idea, though. I was studying another painter. (It took him a moment to remember and it frustrated him.) Matisse. Matisse painted it that way. I was studying his stations. I liked the way he did that.

Caroline: (Again, I was moved to tears and could hardly speak for a moment.) It looks like he's smiling.

Fred: Oh, he is.

Caroline: (I felt on my feet for the first time in this conversation. I actually got something right.) He's smiling, but he doesn't quite look happy. Just sort of happy. (I said this tentatively.)

Fred: He's smiling because he wants to give joy to the world. He wants to give joy to everyone. Not just the people who are there, but he wants to give joy to us, too. Even now, all these years later. He wants to give joy to everyone. Then and now. (Fred's face was very animated as he spoke.) But he's afraid. You can see it in his face. He's afraid of what's going to happen after he dies. He's afraid of what people will do to each other. He's afraid of violence. He's afraid of war.

There was a long moment of silence between us.

Fred: He was right to be afraid.

Another long moment of silence.

Fred: He was right to give us joy, too.

TENTH STATION: JESUS IS STRIPPED OF HIS GARMENTS

For Reflection:

- How might you begin to incorporate the liturgical art of your children into the worshiping life of the whole community?
- What conversation might you have with the artists?
- Again, remember this, a child must know himself to be safe in your church community. The task of the adult is to create and support the matrix out of which this kind of work can come.

Fred:	This one's my favorite. One of them, anyway.
Caroline:	Yeah?
Fred:	Artistically, I think it's the nicest. It's not a just a picture of a soldier stripping Jesus' robe. It's more symbolic.
Caroline:	How so?
Fred:	Well, you don't see Jesus or the soldier. It's not so personal at this point.
Caroline:	How did you decide to do it like that?
Fred:	Well, I was thinking, how do I make this Fred's station, and not Fred copying someone else's station. If it were today, the soldier wouldn't want to show his face. Not then, either. He was ashamed. He was forced to do this. He would not want all the people who loved Jesus to know who he was.

I was thinking about capital punishment. I was thinking about firing squads. I was thinking about our efforts to protect the anonymity of those who are actually involved in the executions.

| Fred: | Maybe he loved Jesus, too. Look how strong his arm is. His hand. That's why I like it so much. |

ELEVENTH STATION: JESUS IS NAILED TO THE CROSS

Fred jumped right in on this one.

Fred:	Same thing. This is good because nobody has to know who's doing the nailing.
Caroline:	An anonymous killing.
Fred:	Yep. You know those pictures of hangmen? They have hoods over their heads? Anonymous like that.

I could tell that Fred likes this painting.

Fred:	You know, there's really two paintings here. One of the hand and one of the hammer. That's what's good about it, because the hand with the hammer doesn't have to be doing something evil.
Caroline:	Are you saying that the hammer hand doesn't have to be the hand of the executioner? That there's some ambiguity in this painting?
Fred:	That's exactly what I'm saying. There's a kind of distance.
Caroline:	I notice that the painting around the hammer is clean. Kind of antiseptic.
Fred:	Everybody washes their hands. Not just Pilate. Everybody but Jesus, anyway.

We looked at Jesus' hand. At the nail and the wound. At the rivers of blood.

TWELFTH STATION: JESUS DIES ON THE CROSS

Caroline:	Jesus looks so small up there. No wonder he fell so many times. His body looks so small.
Fred:	His body really isn't all that important anymore. Actually, he's not altogether human anymore. He's changed. You can see his halo.
Caroline:	Is anybody there? With him?

Fred thought about this for a moment.

Fred: Mary.

Caroline: Mary his mother? She's there?

Fred: Yeah, she's there. Keeping watch. But not too close because it would hurt her too much. And the disciples are there. They're quiet. Especially Peter. He's very quiet. Everybody's praying.

Fred and I were quiet as well.

Fred admitted being bored at times. Once he wanted to quit. We talked about that at length. It was okay that he not finish the series. Finishing it was never the point. The purpose was to discover the kind and depth of spiritual work a child can accomplish, given free reign and an extended period of time.

Fred and I made a contract. "Do one more," I asked him, after a several month hiatus. "And then, if you decide not to do any more, come tell me."

I wanted Fred to be intentional about whether or not he would continue.

He agreed to that. He painted another. Then another. And pretty soon, we were at nine finished.

"I think I can do the rest now," he told me. A short time later he stopped again. "It's too hard," he told me. "The journey itself is too hard."

Fred did not close the story in the tomb.

"I wanted the real ending," he told me. "So I drew the last one with the stone rolled back and the tomb empty."

We hung Fred's stations in the church during Lent, the appropriate reflection taped to the back of each.

Sundays after the services, people spent time with the paintings, spent time with Fred.

On Good Friday we developed focus questions for each step of the journey to accompany the paintings and reflections. For example, "Put yourself in the role of a Roman soldier. Reflect on your own response to the execution of Jesus." Or, "Can you describe a period of growth in your own life, when you, like Fred, found your own gift?"

This project changed Fred's life and mine. It has also enriched the life of the congregation. We learned to value the gifts and contributions of each of us in a new way. The adults became willing to let the children teach them and challenge them to deepen their spiritual lives.

Fred showed all of us a new way to be with one another.

Maybe you have a young artist in your congregation. Perhaps several. Be attentive to the possibilities of spiritual depth that children may bring to the whole community through their art.

Just Start

Just start down this road. That's all that's required of you. It is not possible to imagine or predict, much less control, the surprises of the Spirit as she engages you and your community in the work of conversion and transformation.

Be joyful in the Lord!

Bring together a small group of adults, teens and children. Design a piece of liturgical art and create it. Use it in your sanctuary.

A Spillover Church

I have been blessed by opportunities to design liturgies for conferences, leadership days, ministry fairs, and special community occasions. I have had the privilege of partnerships with people from distinct traditions, diverse cultures, a mix of ages, and different spiritual needs.

I have worked with musicians, composers, vocalists, break dancers, ballet dancers, poets, and painters, all of us committed to the design of liturgies which convert and compel congregations into a few moments of deep response from within the sacred heart of corporate worship.

I have been witness to the movement and quickening of the Spirit on more occasions than I can recount. I have seen lives changed —my own included—by the power of worship.

Yet, invariably, upon the heels of an opening liturgy at a conference, say, or the closing gathering at a diocesan leadership day, people have come to me, sometimes in tears, in twos or in threes, or in a group, "I have loved this. I have come alive. People need to worship like this." I see the struggle. I know what's coming.

"But we could never do this in my church."

This is a hard chapter to write, but I want to acknowledge that the changes I have been discussing can be difficult and painful—liturgies that transform and convert also break hearts.

Many of us will recognize ourselves in the pages that follow.

That's a good thing.

And if we are willing to claim and confess ourselves as the stumbling blocks that we are to the building of inclusive community, then maybe we can learn to laugh gently and to tease each other out of our separate and collective resistance to liturgical change.

Chains of Safety

People speak often of the safety and comfort of familiar liturgies. "Don't change a thing. Church on Sunday is the only safe haven I have." Don't we all know this yearning and longing to have things stay the same?

I have been witness to the movement and quickening of the Spirit on more occasions than I can recount. I have seen lives changed—my own included—by the power of worship.

There is a tension here that is always at play. And the walk along the edge of that tension is not easy. Not only that, there are very few maps.

But there are some points to remember.

- Liturgies that serve the safety and comfort of some people do not serve all people.

- Liturgies that serve the safety and comfort of some people are not liturgies that convert congregations.

- Congregations that are willing to open themselves up to conversion are communities that can find safety in change.

- Personal piety comes into conflict with the spiritual and liturgical needs of a community every day.

These are givens, and so we have to make decisions about them. What matters? What matters the most? Every community will address and resolve those questions in its own way, with its own resources.

Let the bias of this book, however, be clear. Liturgies that serve the safety and comfort of some of the community do not convert the whole community and by definition are exclusive.

The common language we use to evangelize is so often the language of coercion rather than conversion. We welcome you. We want you. Be like us.

We do it to our children. We do it to each other.

Can we reach for a vision of evangelism that assumes that each new person who graces the community will alter the complexion and the spirituality and the depth of the community?

Can we understand this as a good and desirable thing?

Can we understand evangelism in terms of the mutuality of the exchange of the gospel?

Liturgies that carry the seeds of their own evolution are risky. But the greater risk by far, lies in their changelessness.

People seek safety.

But the safety we seek lies not in the inalterability of our liturgies. Our safety lies in God. Our safety lies in our willingness and our capacity to build inclusive communities, communities that worship together, communities open to the possibility of conversion.

A Few Observations

Congregations in general seem to clothe themselves—their ads in the Yellow Pages, local papers, Chamber of Commerce literature—in the language of welcome and hospitality. "Child friendly" is a common phrase, as is "We welcome families."

We are quick to lift up our services of "Family Worship." And yet, within those services of family worship, where are the children? In Sunday school, most likely.

A friend and colleague was interviewing for the position of Director of Family Ministries in a large suburban congregation. She attended the family service, after which she asked the rector, in her words, as innocently as she could manage, "Which of these services is the family service?"

For Reflection:

Can we reach for a vision of evangelism that assumes that each new person who graces the community will alter the complexion and the spirituality and the depth of the community?

"The ten o'clock service. The one you just went to."

"And what time do you offer Sunday school?"

"At ten o'clock."

"And in this family service that I just went to, where were the children?"

"In Sunday school."

In casual conversation or intentional workshops or classes, parents of children will say, "I hated church."

Another will agree. "I couldn't wait until I was old enough to stop going."

Still another might join the conversation, "My mother had to drag me to church."

Pretty soon the energy will intensify.

"My mother used to slap me."

"My sister and I used to have contests—which one of us will be removed first?"

"Who could travel the length of the church underneath the pews?"

"Who could disappear underneath the pews?"

"Who would be the first to faint?"

The laughter that accompanies this conversation and others like it is symptomatic of our inclination to revise history. Being slapped, pinched or removed from church was a shunning and shameful experience at the time, no matter how we dress it up now.

And these are the parents who say with a shrug, "I survived it. My child will survive it."

In one breath, a parent will say, "We had to memorize whole sections of the Bible. I hated it." And in the next breath, she will say, "My children don't seem to be learning much Bible. Maybe if we made them memorize certain passages...."

And the real irony? We convince ourselves that it makes some kind of strange sense.

Not long ago a colleague suggested, "Let's build a big pew. Let's build a pew so big that it will give a person six feet tall the experience of being three feet tall."

He built the pew for the Center for Children at Worship, and that pew made its first formal appearance in March 2000, at the Syracuse, New York conference, "Living the Children's Charter: Transforming Lives."

We developed a dramatic presentation for the opening liturgy, using adults as children. We turned them loose on the pew while a long-winded preacher droned on and on. People laughed so hard they cried. And then they remembered.

"Oh. It was so hard, being made to sit still."

"I couldn't do it."

"It was shameful, being ushered out of church."

"People would always turn around and look at me."

"I know I embarrassed my mother."

And then, the moment came. "Why are we still doing this to our children?"

People resist change. I hear that often. I hear it as a rationale for just about everything liturgical. "We sang a new hymn today. I hate change. Why can't we just sing the ones we know?"

Contemporary hymnody and contemporary prayers carry challenge. New language, new stories confront us. We have to address old issues—racism, sexism, and patriarchy—in new ways. We are confronted by our own participation in these things, and we don't like it.

I wonder sometimes if we don't claim resistance to change so that we don't have to address issues that might lie beneath the resistance.

Contemporary hymnody and contemporary prayers carry challenge. New language, new stories confront us. We have to address old issues—racism, sexism, and patriarchy—in new ways. We are confronted by our own participation in these things, and we don't like it.

A friend speaks of fear. She says, "If we do not hold our mouths just right, say the words just right, create a worshipful atmosphere (whatever that is) God will just not hear us and our efforts at worship will all have been in vain. And we desperately need God's attention. Children distract us and mess up the mood."

We call children a distraction, perhaps, because that was the name given us as children. If we could provide a worship experience that engaged our children, then they wouldn't be distracted. And if we could allow ourselves to entertain a new worship perspective, one that included spontaneous bursts of joy and celebration, that included bodily movement, that included humor and even laughter, then we would no longer be compelled to use the word "distraction." to describe what was happening. We might use the words "Spirit-filled" or "lively" or "celebratory."

Think about this. As children, most adults were excluded or segregated from worship. The message was clear. This is how you do it. If you can't do it this way, and clearly you can't, then you have to leave. And we do leave. For many of us, church was so exclusively adult that we escaped immediately on the heels what many have dubbed the "Graduation Rite", namely Confirmation.

So powerful was the message that when (perhaps "if") we return to church as parents, all we have are those intense, formative moments of our childhood. Our ecclesiology is truncated, reminiscent of an adolescent who never stayed around long enough to do what adolescents are designed to do, namely challenge. And all we can do is that which our parents did, only we try to do it better.

I came back to church following a twenty-year hiatus. Of the three Sunday services offered, I chose the most familiar, because that was the way I had learned it, and, therefore, it was the right way. It was also the most traditional, and the congregation was graying. One Sunday I brought a high school friend, toddler in tow, to this service. That child had a hard time, and so did everyone within the walls of the church. There was pain all around.

Following the service, the rector approached us and suggested to my friend that she might be more comfortable in the nine o'clock service. I believe his words were kindly meant. They were offered gently. And yet I plummeted into early childhood experiences of church where anger and shame and punitive measures were the order of the day.

Talking Tradition

Suppose your pastor told you to expect a traditional Palm Sunday this year. Maybe you wouldn't think much about it because Palm Sunday has always been Palm Sunday, last year's leaflet, this year's date.

But you always begin with the Procession of Palms in the lower parking lot which, as it happens this year, is under construction. Equipment, drain pipes, tape strung from corner to corner...it's a mess. People will trip. People will break bones.

No problem, your pastor explains. She's talking about a traditional Palm Sunday. She plans to gather the congregation on the hilltop to the north of town, read the story of Jesus as he rides into Jerusalem for the last time, bless and distribute branches of palm, and march back into town.

A traditional Palm Sunday celebration. Not Palm Sunday as it hit Spain and Gaul and then seventh-century Rome, not Palm Sunday as it hit the shores of England, not Palm Sunday "as we've always done it," but Palm Sunday as it began, in Jerusalem, two thousand years ago. No reading of the Passion Gospel, of the trial and crucifixion of Jesus. No eucharistic feast claiming the power of the Resurrection. Just a gathering of the people, a simple story, and a procession of palms from a hilltop into a town.

Talking tradition confuses us. What we often call tradition goes by another name. Habit. The way it's always been done in this place. We take the narrow view.

Start Talking

What is it that we're afraid of when we begin to contemplate making the changes in our liturgies that will serve entire communities? Ask that question. Have a conversation. Design it in such a way that people can speak what's on their hearts without censure, without the need to defend, without entrenchment or entrapment or divisiveness.

What does it mean in a service of Baptism to respond as one voice to the question, "Will you who witness these vows do all in your power to support these persons in their life in Christ?" When "these persons" are children, does their participation in the regular worship of the church not matter?

What does it mean to worship as a community when the children and teens aren't present?

Ask the people of your congregation to talk about their theology of community. What matters? What matters the most? And if your answers include the presence of children, ask further questions. Do children participate in worship? Do they participate in the decision making of the congregation? Are their gifts and ministries recognized and exercised?

The conversation is essential. Frame it so that some structure is recognizable, but allow it as great a fluidity as possible. Engage the congregation in this discussion over a period of several months.

You won't reach everyone, so use all means of communication available. Distribute newsletters. Print key questions each week in the service leaflet. Let this discussion inform the agendas of committee meetings. Still, you won't reach everyone, and those you do reach may be unable to arrive at the core of their resistance.

At some point, the leadership of your congregation will have to make decisions, and those decisions, ultimately, will not rise or fall on personal preference, personal piety or general popularity.

The question at its root is "How do we design a liturgy that both serves the people—all the people—and at the same time draws them ever deeper into a love relationship with God and each other?"

Expect to be derailed. Expect the discussion to fall outside the bounds of logic. Liturgy, after all, is—or ought to be—a right-brained experience. Expect heightened emotions.

But hold fast to the vision of inclusive worship. Speak to the vision, with compassion and gentleness and a steadfast resolve.

For Reflection

What is it that we're afraid of when we begin to contemplate making the changes in our liturgies that will serve entire communities?

Worship Design in an Evolutionary World

In the first chapter of this book, I spoke of the irony of bringing this book into containable form at last, only to have it shift like a leaf in a whimsical breeze.

I would like now to return to the opening premise: liturgy of this kind is evolutionary. It grows as the community grows, deepens as the corporate spirituality deepens.

Things will change, and the question you will ask of yourselves again and again, "How will we know when it's time?"

The question won't go away, and the sooner you give it some attention the better. Here's my suggestion. When you hear a call for change, in whatever form it takes, remember Harriet. Remember Harriet on her belly, in the spring woods of Western Pennsylvania.

"Sh-h-h," she's telling us. "Listen. Watch. We'll know it when we see it."

If you are attentive, you will hear the questions and comments. Here's what it sounded like to us.

Our office administrator said to me, "Richard has been writing me e-mail. He wants to know this, regarding our expectations of children in church. 'Do you lower the mountain so that the least of us can scale it, or do you leave the mountain in place so that all of us can aspire to it?'"

Now that's an interesting question.

At one level, liturgies aren't about mountains at all. Liturgies are about relationships: relationship to self; to community; to one another; relationship to God. And liturgies are about expressing those relationships in dynamic and ever-deepening ways.

Still, the question and the imagery calls us to take notice, and as is often the case, Richard's inquiry coincided with a conversation I'd just had with a mother of two children—a four-year-old and a toddler. "It's hard for me to come to church right now," she said. "Even though it's terrific for the children, I need something more."

A comment is made. A door opens. In the light of the conversation with a young mother, Richard's comments about the mountain took on a new dimension, and we began to reconfigure the structure of the service.

Included in Appendix D is a more detailed description of this further piece of our liturgical evolution.

Liturgies are about relationships: relationship to self; to community; to one another; relationship to God. And liturgies are about expressing those relationships in dynamic and ever-deepening ways.

Children in Church: Where to Begin?

Maya Angelou tells a story of her grandmother, "Standing out on the Lord," which was the way her grandmother described her prayer life. Standing out on the Lord.

I picture that as just walking out, taking a step to "but there, somewhere" in air, darkness all around, darkness swirling, nothing under your feet, nothing but God.

Standing out on the Lord, where there is no fear.

Hold that image with you as you begin the work of full inclusion. Bathe yourself in it. Then begin with the theological and practical assumptions that anchor the practical applications you have read in this text. You will likely begin where many of us begin. I call it "accommodation thinking."

"We'll start a children's choir."

"I know. We can let children read the lessons."

"We can have children read the prayers."

"They'll have to practice."

"We won't be able to hear them."

"They'll speak too fast. They always do."

"They can't even reach the lectern."

Where, I wonder, are the voices of the young people in this discussion? Our first questions are about asking children and youth to take on adult roles in adult worship. As I suggested elsewhere in this book, at the root of our willingness to accommodate children is our resistance to the transformation of worship and, ultimately, ourselves.

Accommodating children doesn't work. Accommodating children serves no one. Asking children to function as adults isn't particularly useful, and ultimately, will fail as a strategy for inclusion.

Yet, that's where most of us will start. And that's okay because the important thing is to start.

Here's what will happen.

When children are present, regardless of what the adults are asking them to do, no matter how the adults are trying to control things, there will be surprises. Children and surprises go together. And when there are surprises, there is the context and the promise of conversion. It can't be helped. The Spirit will not go unheeded.

And when a surprise is caught, recognized, there is movement. And when there is movement, there will be an openness to another surprise.

I remember the first time I saw the Vietnam War Memorial, in Washington, D.C.

It was a glorious crisp clear day in early September, and I was on a mission to find the name of an elementary school friend I knew was etched in the wall. I was so intent on finding the wall that I didn't realize it had started at my ankles. I did not know that I was wading down into the experience until I was knee deep, then waist deep. I was so busy looking for the wall that I didn't know I had already found it.

The experience of children in church is like that. Our focus is elsewhere, and so we are surprised. As is most often the case, surprise upon surprise creates the expectation of surprise, and allows us an openness and an eagerness that, in turn, opens us further. Worshiping with the children and youth of a congregation will change—cannot help but change—congregations. It will break our hearts, widen our embrace, dissolve us in laughter and frustration, heal us, break down barriers of age, race, culture, economics, education, sexual orientation, and religious history.

Inclusion is catching.

The active and participating presence of children in the worship life of the community is a conversion experience.

Make the Commitment

Make the commitment to include children as full members of the worshiping community. This is the first step. It's the right decision. It's a necessary decision. How you live out that commitment will vary from congregation to congregation, but the first step is to make that decision. Opt for the gospel inclusion of children.

When children are present, regardless of what the adults are asking them to do, no matter how the adults are trying to control things, there will be surprises. Children and surprises go together.

Then, when you try something and you stumble, which I promise you will happen, you can revise, re-think the particulars and still stay with the commitment. This is critical.

Work from the Assumptions

It is important to lay the theological groundwork for the changes you are about to make. Once is probably not enough. The foundational part of the conversation is continuous. The theological groundwork shapes the pragmatics of worship. But over time, the pragmatics will inform and reshape the theological foundation.

Included here are the working assumptions of the Center for Children at Worship. We recommend them as the foundation for your own work.

- Children belong in church. The children and youth of the worshiping community have as urgent a claim on the space, style, content, and structure of weekly worship as any adult.

- A community is diminished to the extent it is missing the voices of its children and youth. (This is true for the voices of its non-dominant cultures and races, for its elderly, for those marginalized by their gender and/or sexual orientation.)

- Liturgies that evolve as the spirituality of the congregation deepens will serve to convert congregations to the gospel.

- The work, service, education, and decision making of converted congregations will spill over into every aspect of their lives.

- Full inclusion of all people in worship is an issue of justice.

This is a book about children at worship, a book that uses children as the centerpiece of the inquiry. The principles here, however, hold fast no matter what your circumstances. The goal is the ongoing conversion to the gospel.

Use these assumptions as the starting point for congregational education. Talk the big picture. This is not about hospitality to children; it is not about accommodating children in church. This is about bringing near the Kingdom of God.

At the time of this writing, many congregations have lifted out one or two of the ideas in this book and dropped them into their circumstances. The changes are working wonderfully and powerfully for them. Sometimes, however, I hear something different. "We tried the confession stones, but they didn't work," or "We used prayer cards for a while, but they were too much trouble."

It is critical that you lay the theological groundwork. Ask the questions out loud. Why is this important? Why are we doing this? What are the scriptural and theological warrants for confession stones? How might prayer cards strengthen the life of a congregation?

Paint the big picture. The power of the gospel supplants fear and anxiety.

It is important to lay the theological groundwork for the changes you are about to make.

Take Short Steps

Perhaps the decision to include children in regular worship is one that needs to happen in steps.

Start building. This work happens little by little, step by step, year in, year out. Work on the storytelling. Work on your prayer life. Do art. Come to the Table. Teach. Talk to one another.

Make mistakes. Be willing to modify your ideas. Take another step.

Watch how things grow. One Sunday morning it will dawn on you, "We have a program! It's working."

Build What Fits

Hold the ideas presented in this book loosely, especially at first. Know that what is working for one congregation in one part of the country or under one set of demographics may not work for another congregation in other circumstances.

The task of each congregation, I think, is to work from the structures of its own worship. Peel the forms back to the skeleton and rebuild it in a way that includes everybody.

Have conversations with each other about the vision and the practical applications. Don't be afraid to evaluate what you're doing in the light of what you envision.

Experiment! Try things!

Then use, if you wish, any or all of the ideas contained in this book. Consider communicating with the Center for Children at Worship (www.childrenatworship.org) about your experiences. Help build a network of those of us who dream and struggle to find ways to build inclusive gospel communities.

Embrace Conversion

Charles's grandparents brought him to church because his parents wouldn't. He was ten years old, very smart and very troubled.

Charles painted and drew the shape of his psyche. He was not shy about that, and the expression of his psyche was violent. Charles drew explosive pictures of war and destruction: tankers in fiery collision, nuclear bombs, dismembered victims. He drew explosions about to happen. Fighter planes on collision courses in the sky, bombs hanging from their underbellies.

After his initial artistic statements, Charles grew quiet and introspective. He was watchful, attentive.

One day we asked the children to cut poster board in the shape of a heart. We asked them to draw or paint the "Voice of God" as they were hearing it that day.

On his heart, Charles drew a dark chaotic cloud. Inside the cloud, untouched by the penetrating darkness, he placed a circle of light, with glue and gold glitter. And on the back of the card he wrote: "God is the light that cannot be touched, harmed or overtaken by the darkness of the world."

Charles carries that light in his heart. It is the light of Christ who loves him with an unchanging love, and Charles knows that love, knows it deeply.

It is exactly what our children need to know. It is exactly what our children come to know. It's what we all need to know. Sadly, not all of us come this way.

It is no accident that a child like Erin offers her heart's poetry into this community. It is no accident that Missy writes a song and then sings it as her gift to God and to us. It is no accident that Fred spends a year and a half taking a journey with Jesus. And you know that the journey Fred took was the hardest of journeys.

I believe that our goal as people of God, people of Christ, is to challenge each other, allow each other and help each other find and know and live out of the light which is Christ in the world.

A Spillover Church

When I was a child I kept a special book close to my bed. I no longer remember its title, but the story still fills my heart. This is the way I remember it.

An old woman lived alone in a house on the edge of the town. Her children were grown and gone. She was lonely. She invited the children of the community into her house to make popcorn. They all came. The old woman was somewhat forgetful. She was also excited, and in her excitement she put too much popcorn in the popper, and she forgot to put a lid on it.

The popcorn started to pop and it never stopped. Popcorn filled her kitchen, her living room, upstairs in her bedroom, even the attic. Popcorn spilled out the windows into the street. Popcorn spilled out her chimney. Popcorn lifted the roof of her house.

It's a great story. I loved that story, and I read it over and over. The story of children in church has its parallels. It's a spillover story.

What will it look like, your new church? Shut your eyes, for a moment. Take a look.

People are there early, as much as half an hour early. And not just the people in charge.

Children are there, running, laughing. Their parents aren't even in sight. They're still struggling to extract themselves from their cars. You can probably remember when children came to church with little storm clouds hanging over their heads? Wasn't your daughter eleven or twelve when you asked her—made her, if she's telling the story—come to an ecumenical Thanksgiving service. Her eyebrows knit into a permanent scowl; her lip curled, and she kept her arms folded tight across her chest.

These children aren't angry about coming to church.

Inside the doors, a tall skinny kid with braces on this teeth is putting on his vestments. He's the one who got caught throwing oranges at cars. But this same kid completed the training for this lay eucharistic ministry, three consecutive Saturdays. You've watched him serve at the altar before, and you marvel at his presence. Something happens to him, doesn't it, when he offers the chalice to the people of his community, the young ones, old ones, the babies, even his sister, his parents. Something happens. This child knows the awe and the mystery of the sacred moment. He fills the church with his presence and wonder. He is thirteen years old.

I believe that our goal as people of God, people of Christ, is to challenge each other, allow each other and help each other find and know and live out of the light which is Christ in the world.

The two Corbin children have got Margaret Adamson by the skirt. They need her to come out the door with them so they can spill the consecrated wine from the earlier service back to the earth. They're not allowed to touch the wine themselves, so they designate an adult.

The altar guild is cleaning up and setting up; it's a family affair. Even so, you're surprised to see dads and their sons. And you never thought you'd see Mike with an iron in his hand, at least not one that plugs in.

Meggie is standing on the altar rail so she can pour fluid into the standing candles, and Dee is standing there with her. Something in your stomach gives a sudden lurch—it's the altar guild directress in you—and you have to remind yourself to ask, "What's important here?"

There's a child who looks familiar. Where have you seen him before? Now you remember. You saw his face on a poster on Main Street, tacked to a telephone pole. "If you see this child with a cigarette in his mouth, please take it out."

What kind of a community would put up a poster like that? A community that advocates for its children!

The choir is rehearsing, and the anthem is designed for children's voices as well. You like that. It's good that children sing. And you recognize the ten-year-old. She sang a solo last week, the first week of Lent. It was the second song she'd composed and set to music herself. She sang it so beautifully.

The Stations of the Cross that Fred painted line the walls. You've read the reflections about each painting, and you've talked to Fred about his experience. You remember that his reflections formed the basis of the Good Friday liturgy last year. And now, you're told, one of the young parents in the congregation has asked if he can develop the reflections for this year.

Adults and teens are rehearsing a scriptural reading. Bobbie is one of them. You know her well her because she serves with you on the vestry. You're the one who drives her home after the meetings. She's in eighth grade, and the only subject she likes so far this semester is algebra.

Amelia you know, too, because she is the teen chair of the Stewardship Committee.

Maybe you thought that was ill-advised, in the beginning, the decision to invite teens and older children to serve on every decision-making body. After all, they don't know enough, and they haven't had much experience. But you've changed your mind. Meetings are a lot livelier. The work gets done, and in very creative ways. Things are fun. And, funny thing, there doesn't seem to be so much dissention.

You wave to Will and hold up your hiking shoes. Will's the one who takes groups up the mountain, to work on the county-wide restoration project, and today you've made plans to go with him.

People belong here. You know it. They know it.

Even the people you've never seen here before, those two men by the door. Candace and her two children are introducing themselves and making them nametags. Thomas, who had his fourth birthday last month, is offering them prayer cards with colored pens.

It's noisy. It bubbles. The bowl bell sounds. It doesn't exactly get quiet. But you hear the pastor's joyful voice from the back of the church. "Lord! The air smells good today."

The music starts and children accompany the procession with tambourines and drums.

Children make their way to their godparents' laps and the laps of their favorite teens. Parents of children sigh and settle in. Church is beginning, late, of course, and still people straggle in through the doors.

At the pastor's request, in place of the sermon, you have agreed to tell your story of the adoption of your first child. You're a little nervous, but you take comfort in the fact that the baby is with you and lies sleeping in your arms.

There are a lot of prayers today, and the five prayer leaders have divided them up. They read them from their seats, bang bang bang, like little explosions, and after each round of five, the congregation sings a refrain.

It's not getting any quieter. Isn't there a part of you that misses that quiet? Of course there is, but you could have gone to the earlier service. What is it then that keeps bringing you back here? What is it that is so compelling?

Toddlers drop confession stones on the hard wood floor. So does an adult. You smile.

You remember when the stones first arrived. You were there. In the several days between Ash Wednesday and the First Sunday of Lent, you got a frantic phone call from a parent who was sick. "I need help," she told you, and you said yes.

You took children to gather stones, stones the size of a silver dollar. You didn't even know what they were for at the time. But you did as you'd been hastily instructed. You told them the stories of Moses and the people of God in the Desert. Told them of Joshua and the Promised Land, Jesus in the desert after his Baptism. You gave the Rock it's name—the Christ.

You brought the stones into the church and you and the children all blessed them. The children understood that this was their gift to the congregation. You understood your part in the same way.

That first Sunday, after making confession, you were part of that procession to the baptismal font where you dropped the stones in and poured water over them. Do you remember? The stones stayed in the font for the duration of Lent. Each week the congregation added more.

At the Offertory, people of all ages come to the table, gathering around it for the prayer of consecration. You're happy to be watching from the pew, your new baby in your arms. She is gurgling. You marvel at the chaos. How can this be church? Sometimes you shake your head. Lord, help me with my unbelief.

The pastor offers this Holy Communion in honor of the birth and the adoption of your new baby girl. You are overcome with joy and promise. Tears course down your cheeks and fall from your chin onto the baby's head. She looks up at you and smiles, and your heart breaks again.

The children celebrate with the pastor, their hands do what hers do. You see a child who looks very upset. She's starting to cry and she's pulling away, off into the corner. She slides down the wall, squats on her heels, disconsolate. You want to help so you start up there. But before you take a step, the thirteen-year-old tall skinny kid with braces on his teeth has got that child by her hand, which he places on the stem of the chalice. "I need your help here," he tells her, and the two of them make their way along the altar rail, passing the common cup.

You breathe a sigh of relief and amazement, and you move into line to receive.

Is this your church? I'd say so. You belong here, in this spillover church. And you know it.

Appendix A: Children's Charter

CHILDREN'S CHARTER
FOR THE CHURCH

THE EPISCOPAL CHURCH

Nurture of THE CHILD

Children are a heritage from the LORD, and the fruit of the womb is a gift. — Psalm 127:4 (BCP)

THE CHURCH IS CALLED:

* to receive, nurture and treasure each child as a gift from God;
* to proclaim the Gospel to children, in ways that empower them to receive and respond to God's love;
* to give high priority to the quality of planning for children and the preparation and support of those who minister with them;
* to include children, in fulfillment of the Baptismal Covenant, as members and full participants in the Eucharistic community and in the church's common life of prayer, witness and service.

Ministry to THE CHILD

Then Jesus took the children in his arms, placed his hands on each of them and blessed them. — Mark 10:16

THE CHURCH IS CALLED:

* to love, shelter, protect and defend children within its own community and in the world, especially those who are abused, neglected or in danger;
* to nurture and support families in caring for their children, acting in their children's best interest, and recognizing and fostering their children's spirituality and unique gifts;
* to embrace children who seek Christian nurture independently of their parents' participation in the church;
* to advocate for the integrity of childhood and the dignity of all children at every level of our religious, civic and political structures.

Ministry of THE CHILD

A child shall lead them — Isaiah 11:6

THE CHURCH IS CALLED:

* to receive children's special gifts as signs of the Reign of God;
* to foster community beyond the family unit, in which children, youth and adults know each other by name, minister to each other, and are partners together in serving Christ in the world;
* to appreciate children's abilities and readiness to represent Christ and his church, to bear witness to him wherever they may be, and according to gifts given them, to carry on Christ's work of reconciliation in the world, and to take their place in the life, worship, and governance of the church. *(Ministry of the Laity pg. 855 BCP)*

Developed by the Episcopal Dioceses of • Alaska • Bethlehem • Central New York • Chicago • Dallas • Hawaii • Iowa • Massachusetts • Mexico • Southwest Florida • Western North Carolina • Wyoming
• and The Office of Children's Ministries for the Episcopal Church

56-9601-2

Appendix B: Suggested Readings

Alves, Rubem A. *The Poet, the Warrior, the Prophet*. London: SCM Press, 1990.

Bouchard, Dave and Roy Henry Vickers. *The Elders Are Watching*. Golden, Colorado: Fulcrum Publishers, 1993.

> This storyteller and artist together capture the voices and prayers of the Northwest Indians. A powerful book for conversations about peace and justice and the integrity of creation.

Collington, Peter. *A Small Miracle*. New York: Alfred A. Knopf, 1997.

> This is a fabulous Christmas story, a story without words, a story of heartbreak and renewal.

De Paola, Tomie. *Tomie De Paola's Book of Bible Stories*. New York: G. Putnam's Sons, 1990.
———. *Francis: The Poor Man of Assisi*. New York: Holiday House, 1982.
———. *The Miracles of Jesus*. New York: Holiday House, 1996.

> In my opinion, there is nothing that Tomie de Paola doesn't do well. His ability to tell the story and his artistic genius make his work compelling.

Dix, Dom Gregory. *The Shape of Liturgy*. London: Dacre Press, 1945.

Domestic and Foreign Missionary Society (PECUSA). *Called to Teach and Learn*. New York, 1994.

Eckhart, Meister. *Breakthrough: Meister Eckhart's Creation Spirituality*. Introduction and Commentaries by Matthew Fox. Garden City, New York: Image Books, 1980.

Fox, Matthew. *In the Beginning There Was Joy*. Illustrated by Jane Tattersfield. New York: Crossroad, 1995.

> This is a creation story we read over and over.

Hamilton, Virginia, editor and Barry Moser, artist. *In The Beginning: Creation Stories from Around the World*. San Diego: Harcourt Brace Jovanovich, 1998.

Resources:
- Resources come from many places, peoples, publishers and traditions.
- Exploration and discovery is the source of delight for creative work.
- Never underestimate the power of a new resource to spark creative response.

I have found this to be an invaluable compendium of creation myths. Useful in storytelling, drama, multiculturalism.

Handel, George Frederick. *Messiah: The Wordbook for the Oratorio.* Paintings by Barry Moser. San Francisco: A Willa Perlman book from HarperCollins, 1992.

The artist, Barry Moser, brings awe and wonder to Handel's Messiah.

Heine, Helme. *Friends.* New York: Atheneum, 1984.

The illustrations provide the magic for this simple story of friendships within a diverse community. Helme creates a lovely sense of acceptance and play.

——. *The Pearl.* New York: Atheneum, 1985.

Again, with lovely artwork, Helme makes a strong statement about the priority of relationship.

Hickman, Martha and Guiliano Ferri. *And God Created Squash.* Morton Grove, Illinois: Albert Whitman & Co., 1996.

I appreciate the whimsy of this book and the art, even the whimsical white-bearded old man God.

Hodges, Margaret. *St. Jerome and the Lion.* Illustrated by Barry Moser. New York: Orchard Books, 1991.

Barry Moser's art makes a powerful story even more powerful.

Law, Eric H. F. *The Gift of Diversity.* Chalice Press.

L'Engle, Madeleine. *The Glorious Impossible.* New York: Simon & Schuster, 1990.

I like L'Engle's books very much, and recommend them to you. This one is a telling of the Jesus story which I find particularly compelling.

Lionni, Leo. *An Extraordinary Egg.* New York: Alfred A. Knopf, 1994.

I like this whimsical story about a mistaken identity and the discovery of self.

Locker, Thomas. *Water Dance.* San Diego, New York, London: Harcourt, Brace & Company, 1997.

Sasso, Sandy Eisenberg. *But God Remembered.* Illustrated by Bethanne Anderson. Woodstock, Vermont: Jewish Lights Publishing, 1995.

Resource Library:
- Develop your own resource library from which members of the parish may draw inspiration.
- From time to time take children, teachers and members through that library.
- Demonstrate its usefulness.

Sandy Sasso is the kind of theologian you want at your finger-tips. She knows how to build inclusive communities.

———. *God's Paintbrush*. Illustrated by Annette C. Compton. Wood-stock, Vermont: Jewish Lights Publishing, 1992.

These are great reflection opportunities for young people, with study questions designed for Jews and Christians both. This is a valuable resource.

———. *In God's Name*. Woodstock, Vermont: Jewish Lights Publishing, 1994.

It is rare that we discover a writer / theologian so inclusive.

———. *A Prayer for the Earth: The Story of Naaman, Noah's Wife*. Illus-trated by Bethanne Anderson. Woodstock, Vermont: Jewish Lights Publishing, 1996.

Rabbi Sasso remembers the women so long-forgotten. Naaman is one.

Scharper, Philip and Sally. *The Gospel in Art by the Peasants of Solenti-name*. Maryknoll, New York: Orbis Books, 1984.

This is an old favorite of mine, gospel stories in informal conver-sations from the perspective of liberation theology.

Silverstein, Shel. *The Giving Tree*. San Francisco: HarperCollins, 1986.

If ever there was a book about sacrificial giving, this is it. There is an ecological subtext to this story which you may find useful as well.

Stewart, Sonja M. and Jerome Berryman. *Young Children and Wor-ship*. Louisville, Kentucky: Westminster/John Knox Press, 1989.

Strong, Diana and Donald Cook. *Hosanna and Alleluia*. Denver, Colo-rado: Spindle Press.

This is an oversized book, with very good art, that tackles the mysteries of Holy Week and Easter. I recommend this book for any of the Holy Week conversations you have with your chil-dren.

Vavra, Robert and Fleur Cowles. *Lion and Blue*. New York: William Morrow & Co., 1974.

This is my all-time favorite book whose story and painting cap-ture the essence of spiritual journey.

For Reflection:

- Think of a time or a place when you have been ener-gized by a new discovery in a book, or in some interesting state-ment that fits like a piece to some puzzle inside of you.
- How has it ener-gized your work?
- Isn't working from your passion, your discoveries, the most life-giving work you can possibly do?

Vivas, Julie. *The Nativity*. San Diego: Harcourt Brace Jovanovich, 1986.

> You have to have this book, and you have to use it, Christmas after Christmas.

Weisner, David. *Tuesday*. New York: Clarion Books, 1991.

> I use this book when any of the Egyptian plague scripture appears. It has a playful absurdity, and is just ominous enough without being frightening.

Williams, Margery. *The Velveteen Rabbit*. New York: Doubleday, 1958.

> This is a great old story about real love.

Wood, Douglas and Cheng-Khee Chee. *Old Turtle*. Duluth, Minnesota: Pfeifer-Hamilton, 1992.

> This is a great story with great art about the voice of wisdom as it breaks into a violent and chaotic world.

Young, Ed. *Genesis*. San Francisco: Laura Geringer Imprint of Harper-Collins, 1997.

> The creation art in this book is worth having at your side anytime you tell a creation story.

Dr. Seuss. *Horton Hears a Who*. New York: Random House, 1954.

> This is a particularly good Seuss book, I think, because it raises concern for the least of us. It is a call to attentiveness. Many of the Dr. Seuss books lend themselves to good religious discussion. It would be of value to take a look at them.

The Peace

The Liturgy of the Table

This Communion is open to all who desire
to receive Christ in their hearts.
Communicants may come forward, standing, and receive the bread and wine.
To those who desire to receive a blessing only, please cross your arms across your chest.
A few moments of silence will follow.

Offertory Hymn 83, "Just a Little Talk with Jesus," *Lift Every Voice and Sing II,* Church Publishing Incorporated, 1993.

Leader the	The grace of our Lord Jesus Christ and the love of God and the fellowship of the Holy Spirit be with you all.
People	And also with you.
Leader	Lift up your hearts.
People	We lift them to the Lord.
Leader	Let us give thanks to the Lord our God.
People	It is right to give God thanks and praise.

Sanctus
Holy, holy, holy Lord, God of power and might,
Heaven and earth are full of your glory
Hosannah in the highest.
Blessed is he who comes in the name of the Lord.
Hosannah in the highest.

We give thanks...
We break bread...
We remember Jesus...
We receive the Holy Spirit.

The Lord's Prayer

Our Father, who art in heaven,
hallowed be thy Name,
thy kingdom come,
thy will be done,
on earth as it is in heaven.
Give us this day our daily bread.
And forgive us our trespasses,
as we forgive those who trespass against us.
And lead us not into temptation, but deliver us from evil.
For thine is the kingdom, and the power, and the glory,
for ever and ever. Amen

Fraction

Christ our Passover is sacrificed for us.
Therefore let us keep the feast. Alleluia.

Postcommunion Prayer (standing)

Almighty God, giver of all good things,
we thank you for feeding us with the spiritual food
of the precious body and blood of our Savior, Jesus Christ.
We thank you for your love and care
in assuring us of your gift of eternal life
and uniting us with the blessed company
of all faithful people.
Therefore, everliving God,
keep us steadfast in your holy fellowship.
And now we offer ourselves, all that we have and are,
to serve you faithfully in the world,
through Jesus Christ our Redeemer,
to whom with you and the Holy Spirit
be all honor and glory, now and for ever. Amen.

Blessing

Hymn 751, "Every Time I Feel the Spirit," *Wonder, Love, and Praise*, Church Publishing Incorporated, 1997.

Dismissal And God saw everything that He had made, and found it very good. God said, This is the last world I shall make. I place it in your hands. Hold it in trust.
Thanks be to God!

Please be seated for the announcements.

HOLY FAMILY EPISCOPAL CHURCH
1590 S. Cabrillo Highway
Half Moon Bay, CA 94019
(650) 726-0506
The Rev. Caroline S. Fairless, Vicar
Ninth Sunday after Pentecost
August 2, 1998

Family Style

We welcome you to Holy Family Episcopal Church and the Family Service. We're committed to the spiritual growth and nurture of the children of the coastside, and you'll see that commitment reflected in this service. The children set up the worship space for this service. They participate in the Liturgy of the Word, the writing of the Prayers of the People, the Confession, and most of all, the shared Communion of Christ. Following the communion, the children are invited to the classrooms to express in art forms the worship experience they've just had. We're proud of the spiritual and educational opportunities we offer to our children, and again, welcome. We're happy you've joined us.

Acclamation: If you have been raised with Christ, seek the things that are above.

People:　　　Then you also will be revealed with him in glory.

Hymn 542, "Christ is the world's true Light," *The Hymnal 1982,* Church Publishing Incorporated.

Gathering Prayer
Lord, you told us not to worry about tomorrow,
which brings worries of its own.
Help us to love right now for You. Amen.

Song of Praise　　　　　　　　　　　　　　　　711

Share the Good News
How Much is Enough?

Prayers of the Gathered
(All children and adults are invited to express
the desires and thanksgivings of their hearts on the prayer cards provided.)

Confession

God of mercy,
we have done things against you
and against each other.
We have harmed the earth and its creatures.
We are sorry.
We are truly sorry
and we ask your forgiveness.
Help us walk in the way of your love. Amen.

Hymn   A New Heart

A new heart I'll give to you,
A new spirit I will put within you,
And I'll take out of your flesh the heart of stone
And give you a heart of flesh.

Words of Forgiveness

Almighty God have mercy on us, forgive us all your sins through our Lord Jesus Christ,
strengthen us in all goodness, and by the power of the Holy Spirit keep us in eternal life.
Amen.

The Peace

The Liturgy of the Table

> This Communion is open to all who desire
> to receive Christ in their hearts.
> Communicants may come forward, standing, and
> receive the bread and wine.
> To those who desire to receive a blessing only,
> please cross your arms across your chest.
> A few moments of silence will follow.

Hymn 707, "Take my life, and let it be," *The Hymnal 1982,* Church Publishing
Incorporated.

Leader	The grace of our Lord Jesus Christ and the love of God and the fellowship of the Holy Spirit be with you all.
People	And also with you.
Leader	Lift up your hearts.
People	We lift them to the Lord.
Leader	Let us give thanks to the Lord our God.
People	It is right to give God thanks and praise.

Sanctus

Holy, holy, holy Lord, God of power and might,
Heaven and earth are full of your glory
Hosannah in the highest.
Blessed is he who comes in the name of the Lord.
Hosannah in the highest.

> We give thanks...
> We break bread...
> We remember Jesus...
> We receive the Holy Spirit.

THE LORD'S PRAYER
Our Father, who art in heaven,
hallowed be thy Name,
thy kingdom come,
thy will be done,
on earth as it is in heaven.
Give us this day our daily bread.
And forgive us our trespasses,
as we forgive those who trespass against us.
And lead us not into temptation, but deliver us from evil.
For thine is the kingdom, and the power, and the glory,
for ever and ever. Amen

Hymn 151, "One bread, one body," *Lift Every Voice and Sing II*, Church Publishing Incorporated, 1993.

Reader   The Holy Gospel of our Lord Jesus Christ according to Luke.
People   Glory to you, Lord Christ.

The Gospel   Luke 12:13–21

Someone in the crowd said to him, "Teacher, tell my brother to divide the family inheritance with me." But he said to him, "Friend, who set me to be a judge or arbitrator over you?" And he said to them, "Take care! Be on your guard against all kinds of greed; for one's life does not consist in the abundance of possessions." Then he told them a parable: "The land of a rich man produced abundantly. And he thought to himself, 'What should I do, for I have no place to store my crops?' Then he said, 'I will do this: I will pull down my barns and build larger ones, and there I will store all my grain and my goods. And I will say to my soul, "Soul, you have ample goods laid up for many years; relax, eat, drink, be merry." But God said to him, 'You fool! This very night your life is being demanded of you. And the things you have prepared, whose will they be?' So it is with those who store up treasures for themselves but are not rich toward God."

Reader   The Gospel of the Lord.
People   Praise to you, Lord Christ.

Sermon   **The Rev. Caroline S. Fairless**
(A few moments of silence will follow.)

Anthem   **Choir voices**

Postcommunion Prayer (kneeling or standing)
Almighty God, giver of all good things,
we thank you for feeding us with the spiritual food
of the precious body and blood of our Savior, Jesus Christ.
We thank you for your love and care
in assuring us of your gift of eternal life
and uniting us with the blessed company
of all faithful people.

Therefore, everliving God,
keep us steadfast in your holy fellowship.
And now we offer ourselves, all that we have and are,
to serve you faithfully in the world,
through Jesus Christ our Redeemer,
to whom with you and the Holy Spirit
be all honor and glory, now and for ever. Amen.

Blessing

Hymn 550, "Jesus calls us; o'er the tumult," *The Hymnal 1982*, Church Publishing Incorporated.

Dismissal Christ is all and is in all! Let us go forth in His name, rejoicing in the power of the Spirit.
Thanks be to God!

Appendix D: Evolutionary Liturgy

When Richard, a thoughtful member of Holy Family Church, asked this question regarding children in church, "Do you lower the mountain to accommodate the children, or do you keep the mountain at its height and encourage the children to aspire to it," we found the image useful, and began to play with it.

As we began to use the visual piece to describe the structure of what we were doing, it became an easy enough task to shift the energy and focus somewhat, without letting go of the things of value.

We used the illustration below to describe to the congregation how we intended to build in adult reflection and prayer time following Holy Communion.

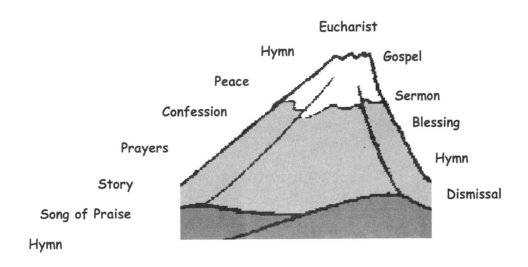

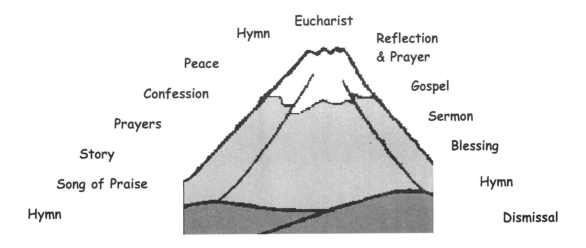